LOST, HIDDEN, SMALL

Praise for *Lost, Hidden, Small*

"I loved this book for its wisdom, message and welcome, its depth and its many charms, especially the clear and deeply human voice of the author, Pastor Kate."

—**Anne Lamott**, *New York Times* bestselling author

"I have had the pleasure of being Kate Murphy's friend for nearly a quarter century. A conversation with Kate always makes me feel selfish. I know that I am not the only person who needs her deep pastoral and scriptural wisdom, wicked humor, and poetic sensibility. You have in your hands the gift of a conversation with one of our finest pastors. She means to change your mind about whom to value and what to value if you have cast your lot with that strange healer, exorcist, and preacher we call Jesus. Our world is being turned upside down before us. Kate means to do the same, but in the interest of beauty, humanity, and the fulfillment of God's dream for creation. May it be so."

—**Rev. Dr. William H. Lamar IV**, pastor of Metropolitan AME Church and author of *Ancestors*

"Kate Haynes Murphy is a kind shepherd—and she is also a storyteller who kindles flames that fan into fire, burning down the illusions we've built around our faith, our lives, and God. With reckless abandon, she enchants us to reimagine the way we see Christ, the way we see others, and—especially—the way we see ourselves. In *Lost, Hidden, Small,* she dares us to forsake all we ever thought we knew for the sake of facing the truth of our lostness . . . and finding the One we can never lose."

—**Rachel Marie Kang**, author of *Let There Be Art* and *The Matter of Little Losses,* and founder of The Fallow House

"Walter Brueggemann has written about how the true work of ministry is rejecting the dominant cultural script—what he calls therapeutic, technological, consumeristic militarism—and living by the counter-script of God. Kate Haynes Murphy casts a similar vision and invites us to embrace an appropriately uncomfortable counter-script that challenges typical American ways of viewing church. Murphy vulnerably recounts her own faith and leadership journey; the temptation to desire a church that is large, in charge, and the talk of the town; and the humbling discovery that the way of Jesus often leads in the opposite direction. This book is an honest and encouraging saga of how someone who feels like a train wreck can participate in the subversive script and ministry of God. It's an invitation to find kinship and delight in the league of holy losers."

—**Wesley Vander Lugt**, theologian and author of *Beauty Is Oxygen: Finding a Faith That Breathes*

KATE HAYNES MURPHY

LOST, HIDDEN, SMALL

FINDING THE WAY OF JESUS WHERE WE NEVER THINK TO LOOK

Broadleaf Books
Minneapolis

LOST, HIDDEN, SMALL
Finding the Way of Jesus Where We Never Think to Look

30 29 28 27 26 25 1 2 3 4 5 6 7 8 9

Details in some anecdotes and stories have been changed to protect the identities and privacy of the persons involved.

Library of Congress Control Number: 2025938369 (print)

Cover design: Broadleaf Books
Cover image: © 2025 Getty Images; US coins/92890281 by TokenPhoto; © 2025 Getty Images; 1 cent coin (back)/200491325-001 by Michael Diva

Print ISBN: 979-8-8898-3700-8
eBook ISBN: 979-8-8898-3701-5

For Colin

CONTENTS

PREFACE

IT STARTED TO rain as I was walking home after dropping my daughter off at kindergarten. It was early spring, warm already in North Carolina, and it was a slow, gentle rain, almost pleasant. I wasn't in a particular hurry, and I hadn't gotten myself ready for work yet. That rain shouldn't have been the thing that pushed me over the edge.

In the last year, the church I served committed to a redevelopment process. Designed by consultants that our denomination had hired, it was billed as a last chance at survival. My first chance at pastoring was the congregation's last chance at surviving. The church I served was hardly unique. Mainline Protestant denominations like mine had been hemorrhaging members for decades. Clearly, the way we knew to "do church" wasn't working anymore. For me, "redevelopment" looked like hours and hours of reading and lectures from evangelical Baptist pastors who had experience growing churches—but didn't believe women were called to ministry. It was learning that everything I didn't know how to do was *essential* and that everything I loved would have to change.

The redevelopment process culminated in The Prescription: a six-page, single-spaced document detailing all the changes our church would have to make to survive, with new name, new leadership structure, new worship style, new ministries, new evangelism strategies. (Which is misleading, as it implies there was an old evangelism strategy. There wasn't. We are Presbyterians.)

After they had read The Prescription, one-third of the sixty-member congregation left.

After beginning, badly, to try and implement it, another third of the congregation walked out—along with a beloved staff member who told everyone she'd been fired. By me.

Days later our presbytery, the institution sponsoring the process, dropped out. Then a larger church we were in the process of merging with canceled the process, explaining that the opportunity costs were too high.

So that left one-third of an almost entirely white congregation, average age sixty-five, within a diverse urban neighborhood, trying to lead a transformation process without any support. My own children were the only ones left under age ten. When I had arrived there three years earlier, there were a few little kids in the church. Their mothers became my closest friends, but those families left too.

Every Sunday, my kids asked me why their friends didn't come anymore. Every Sunday, I struggled to spin a good answer. We'd halved the budget, halved my salary, ended my benefits, and doubled my job description. There'd be no more musicians, no more administrative assistant ("Well, you don't need one with a congregation *that* small," a friend consoled me). I'd pulled my youngest out of day care, my oldest out of after-school care.

I told myself that no matter what happened, it would be okay. I told myself that I'd never regret having more time at home with the kids. I told myself that things would get better. I told myself that it would be fine, that it already *was* fine. I told myself these things again and again, to drown out my internal panic and despair, because I knew this was over. Not just this church, but any church for me. Who would hire the woman who closed the first church she ever pastored?

But it was fine. Everything was fine! I was fine. That was my mantra.

And then, that spring day, it started to rain. That was the moment I stopped telling myself it was fine.

There's a huge flat rock in our yard. That morning, instead of rushing past it to get inside and get another day started, I laid down on the rock. I can't tell you why I did it. I've never laid on a rock before or since. Looking back, I wonder if this is what it looks like to be "slain in the Spirit." All I know is I'd been stoically carrying on for so long because I thought that was what good Christians did: Swallow the pain, the shame, and the fear because good Christians didn't feel that way. Ever. I kept going because I knew that if I stopped to feel any of it, I'd be swallowed in despair. And then it started to rain, and I just couldn't go on going on.

I stayed there, flat on my back on the rock in the rain, just letting myself get soaked in the truth: I was pathetic. I was the loser pastor of a failing, dying, losing church. The only thing more pathetic than sucking at everything is to remain committed to doing things you suck at. The only thing even worse than *that* is to do those things publicly. Loser pastors like me gather a small group of people to watch us suck at everything once a week. Quitting was the only reasonable, face-saving option.

But if I quit, I'd be done forever. And not just with pastoring but with God. Not because I wanted to be, but because every time I entered a sanctuary, it would bring me back to this moment. This moment on the rock in the rain, when I realized that I'd given everything I had—everything I was—to the Lord, and the Lord gave it back. I was frozen on a pathetic rock. I couldn't let go. I couldn't hold on.

So I tapped out.

And that was the moment I began to come alive.

INTRODUCTION

THE SPOTTED LANTERNFLY looks like it's been designed as part of an haute-couture collection. It looks like it belongs in an art museum. When a large flying insect, something that usually disgusts and terrifies, manages instead to be a thing of wonder, its allure is intensified. A lanternfly is astonishing—with its vibrant hues and interlocking, sculpted wings, it's the kind of creature you expect to see in a David Attenborough documentary about an unspoiled, wild place. When you see it in real life, you can't help but marvel that such a thing exists at all, let alone in your neighborhood.

Slowly, and then all at once during the first pandemic summer of 2020, lanternflies were everywhere in New York City, clinging to the sides of buildings, garbage cans, and delivery trucks, subtly nestled on the bark of trees. The ordinary urban landscape became infested with the extraordinary. Lanternflies do not sting or bite. They don't eat flowers or strip leaves from trees. When they move on, they leave no visible trace. They appeared out of nowhere and appeared to exist simply to inspire awe. Their beauty was a reminder that life was still good.

And then the warnings began. New York City was flooded with leaflets and posters depicting the exquisite creature with a shocking command: "If You See This Beautiful Creature, Kill It Immediately," "Die, Beautiful Lantern Fly, Die," and "KILL THEM ALL." Because, as our neighbors to the north discovered years ago, this double-winged beauty was an ecological catastrophe.

Lanternflies feed on sap, the lifeblood of a plant. They leave the external structure pristine while destroying the plant from the inside out. But they don't just suck out sap; they also excrete a sticky substance known as honeydew. Mostly imperceptible to humans, honeydew spawns large colonies of mold. Over time, this sooty mold grows cancer like and covers the surface of leaves, preventing photosynthesis. The lanternflies' lethality is intensified because the damage they cause is invisible until it is catastrophic. In China, where lanternflies are native, the population is kept in balance by voracious wasps. In North America, the species has no predators, and it becomes an annihilating force.

The appearance of lanternflies also intensifies their threat. Humans find it hard to resist anything that is beautiful. If it looks good, it's hard to imagine it might not be good. We look at the outward appearance of a thing and extrapolate interiority. Lanternfly infestations are hard to control, partly because humans have an innate inability to perceive danger in what attracts us. How could anything so lovely be a threat?

But left unchecked, the lanternfly population will decimate almost anything green. They destroy the trees providing the air we breathe, the plants producing the food we eat, and the vines responsible for the wine we drink. Still, we are enthralled by their beauty. We cannot comprehend the danger in a creature so exquisite.

We are ever blinded by our sight.

* * *

This is a book about seeing.

I am a follower of Jesus. When Christians talk about Jesus, we call him many things: Son of God, Shepherd, King of kings, Lion, Lamb, and Lord, but we worship him as our Savior.* When Jesus began his public ministry, he started by declaring himself the source of

---

* The Bible is delightfully, intentionally inclusive when describing God. Scripture describes God as Father, but also as Mother and birth giver. Throughout this book, I use male, female, and nongendered pronouns to refer to God to accurately reflect the diversity of scriptural representation. I use he/him pronouns when referring to Jesus of Nazareth.

freedom and salvation in life (not just after death, as many Christians emphasize). Jesus announced his kingdom mission in a sermon in his local synagogue. They handed him the Torah scroll, and he unrolled it, choosing for himself a passage from the prophet Isaiah. He declared that the spirit of God was upon him to do five things—bring good news to the poor, liberate the captives, recover the sight of the blind, lift the burdens of the oppressed, and proclaim the year of the Lord's favor. These are promises of deliverance for people who are suffering. Jesus announced salvation not somewhere else in the future but here and now, in this life. He concluded his sermon by declaring, "Today this scripture is fulfilled in your hearing" (Luke 4:21).

Jesus's third promise, recovery of sight to the blind, is a declaration of healing. It is an altogether different kind of promise. All the other components of Jesus's mission are external. Good news comes to the poor, prisoners are liberated from captivity, burdens are lifted off the oppressed, and the year of God's favor falls upon the people. But recovery of sight is an internal process. Here Jesus is talking about not something that happens *to* us but something that happens *within* us.

Recovering sight is at the very center of Jesus's mission. It's a spiritual transformation he offers all of us, regardless of how well we believe we can see. In fact, those who think they can already see are the ones who need sight recovery most. In restoring the sight of the blind, Jesus is naming the spiritual catalyst that makes all the other things on the list possible. When the blind recover their sight, it will be good news to the poor. Sighted people will bring liberty to the captives. They will lift off the burdens that oppress their siblings. They will die to who they used to be and be born again as conduits through which God's favor flows.

All four Gospels tell stories of Jesus restoring the ability to see to individuals who are blind. But Jesus is not ableist. He does not believe people who are blind are cursed or deficient or less worthy than sighted people. Physical sight is not essential to Jesus. His mission is to open all people's *spiritual* eyes. He is born to change the way humans see. As he says in John after healing a man born blind, "For judgment I have come into this world, so that the blind will see and those who see will become blind" (John 9:39).

Judgment is one of those words we either weaponize or toss away completely. But Jesus came to restore our sight and judgment inevitably proceeds from clear-sightedness. Not the wrath of God directed against us, but the gift of discernment. Jesus came to restore our sight, which in turn heals our misperceptions and gives us right understanding and the gift of accurate perception.

When I was in my first year of seminary, I called my father complaining about a preaching assignment I considered busy work. The professor had asked us to define several common words in a Scripture passage we were studying. I was annoyed. I wanted to preach, not think about preaching. Indignantly, I told my dad I had better things to do.

He asked me what the words were, and, eager to show off how ridiculously obvious they were, I told him they were simple basic words like *judge* and *judgment*. My father asked me to tell him, since it was so obvious to me, the definition of these words.

I should mention at this point that my father was a lawyer, more specifically a courtroom litigator. I should have sensed the trap in his question, but I was twenty-two and nobody could tell me anything. I huffed impatiently, "Obviously, judgments are decisions and judges are people who make judgments."

I knew from the long pause that followed that I had stepped in it somehow. I can still hear the timbre of his voice as he answered "Oh Katy, everyone makes judgments, all people make decisions and choices all the time. But a judge (pause to build anticipation), a judge is someone whose judgments really matter."

When I think about Jesus as the judge of the world, I no longer picture a viciously indifferent, cosmic force deciding my destiny from behind a bench. I see the humble, homeless healer born into scandal, who spent his infancy as a refugee and as an adult was falsely indicted, unjustly condemned, and executed by the state. This man is the King of kings reigning in the kingdom of God. For me, he is the One whose judgment really matters.

* * *

From a mountaintop vista, Jesus begins to restore our sight by teaching us: "Blessed are the poor in spirit . . . Blessed are those who mourn . . . Blessed are the meek . . . Blessed are those who hunger and thirst for righteousness . . . Blessed are the merciful . . . Blessed are the pure in heart . . . Blessed are the peacemakers . . . Blessed are those who are persecuted . . . Blessed are you when people insult you, persecute you and falsely say all kinds of evil against you because of me" (Matt 5:3–11).

For me, Jesus is the sacred and supreme judge of reality, the One who accurately perceives what is good, the One who can teach me, can teach all of us, how to tell the difference between what appears beautiful and what actually is. Jesus is the One who shows us the gap between what righteousness looks like and what righteousness *is.* I believe Jesus came to restore sight so that we can perceive, choose, and then live in truth that transforms and heals, reconciles and redeems. But before we gain our spiritual sightedness, the way of Jesus does not look like salvation. To those who are spiritually blind, the way of Jesus looks like weak, dangerous, self-destructive foolishness.

Jesus came to restore sight because most of us are spiritually blind. We see lies as truth. We see threats as beautiful. We put our trust in the power to harm, the power to take, and the power to control instead of the powers of healing, generosity, and acceptance. Jesus gives us holy judgment and a vision for a way of living that is so unimaginable and contrary to what most consider "normal" and "sacred" that some Christians have come to call the realm of God the "upside-down kingdom."

It's not just that things, through Jesus's eyes, are not what they seem; it's that they are the very opposite of what they seem. With Jesus, it is always a question of seeing. Not like *that,* but like *this.* A healthy leader doesn't rule from a throne; she kneels to wash feet. A good king isn't served by his minions; he serves like a shepherd. God is not a cosmic threat hurling punishment down from on high but a mother hen sheltering her chicks from the storm.

A life of faith is a life of unlearning our certainty, embracing wonder, and piercing the familiarity that blinds us. Life with Jesus is learning to see as Jesus sees.

And here's the thing: On the Jesus Way, sight precedes salvation. Not because we are unworthy until we see, but because until we see, we cannot perceive what worthiness is. Until we see, salvation looks like destruction, and what is sacred looks like garbage. But hang out with Christ, and you begin to see things differently. Grace sanctifies our eyes. "I was blind but now I see," the old song goes. And seeing, we enter into the kingdom, stunned to realize it is already in our midst.

But first we must realize: Everything beautiful isn't.

* * *

I am fascinated by the lanternfly, by my own reaction to it. I know how dangerous and destructive it is, and yet I can't help marveling at its appearance. How ominous that that which consumes and destroys is attractive to me. If I saw a lanternfly, even given everything I know about its power to annihilate, I would struggle to kill it. Its beauty blinds me to its danger. Its loveliness masks and compounds its lethality.

The lanternfly, an invasive species, is the perfect entomological metaphor for much of the dominant Christian church, what I call the Christian industrial complex. An invasive ideology has corrupted the revelation of Jesus. It is identified by many different labels: white Christian nationalism, consumer Christianity, colonized Christianity, empire Christianity, and more. Whatever we call it, its essence is the same. The Christian industrial complex is an invasive ideology that says anyone who is faithful to Christ will be powerful, wealthy, and revered. It teaches Christians that whatever is centered, celebrated, and large in our culture is a movement of God. It announces that Jesus is at work in the existing dominant power structures and systems of this world. As a result of this invasive ideology, the North American church has an idolatrous obsession with power, size, and reputation. We can't perceive anything else as beautiful.

Instead of crying out with all creation for healing and total redemption, the infected church is confident that the kingdom of Jesus will be made manifest through slight adjustments to the world as it is. Justice will be delivered through the extant justice system and contemporary civil law code. The world's militaries can establish and will maintain global peace. Terrorism can be bombed away. The marketplace will equitably distribute abundance and prosperity. Charity and philanthropy will restore and repair historic harms. These are all idolatrous lies.

This false gospel teaches us to follow Jesus by making ourselves great. It teaches that Jesus empowers us to seize control of powerful institutions. It preaches that we can find Jesus in the consensus of the center. It identifies Jesus's anointing on whoever attracts the largest crowds. Whatever is large, whatever is centered, whatever is celebrated, we think on these things because they are beautiful and excellent in our sight. We declare Jesus's sovereignty is in them. We assume whatever appeals to us must be holy.

Before Jesus began his public ministry, the Gospels say he spent forty days fasting in the desert. In Matthew and Luke, we read that, at the end of that fast, the devil himself comes to seduce Jesus and offer him another way, a more appealing way of being the Son of God. Acknowledging his hunger, Satan encouraged Jesus to feed himself. "If you really are the Son of God, tell these stones that you made to become bread. Use your sacred identity to meet your own needs. Refashion the world around you so that it satisfies your own wants." In other words, center yourself.

Next, Satan takes Jesus to the highest point of the holy city and dares him to throw himself down. "If you really are God's son, Scripture says that his angels will lift you up, will keep you from even stubbing your toe on a rock. The people below will see your miraculous feat and then they will know that you are God's son." In other words, if you are God's Son, perform a spectacular feat the world will celebrate.

Finally, Satan offers Jesus power and authority over every human institution, ownership of every kingdom and realm: "All of this I will give to you, if you will just worship me, if you will walk my way." The devil offers Jesus what is most attractive to the human ego: a large, centered, and celebrated life.

Jesus rejected the devil's beautiful temptations. The church has not been so faithful.

More and more of us are beginning to see, through shame and despair, that our version of faith is the toxic excrement of spiritual lanternflies. We saw political power, large legacy institutions, and public approval as beautiful, and we deemed orthodox any religion that produced what we desired. As a result, much of the spirituality we invested in has left the vine putrid and rotting. The sacred has been sucked out of our institutions, and the mold has set in. We are realizing, in horror, that we have been worshiping and adoring our own destruction. We can no longer trust our own eyes.

There is another way of seeing, of being, and of living. A way that appears neither beautiful nor possible but is both. "Enter through the narrow gate," Jesus said. "For wide is the gate and broad is the road that leads to destruction, and many enter through it. But small is the gate and narrow the road that leads to life, and only a few find it" (Matt 7:13–14).

This is the lost, hidden, and small way of Jesus. It does not lead us to the life we imagined. We are not naturally attracted to the way of Jesus. But the way of lost, hidden, and small leads to the kingdom of God where we inherit a life that is beautiful and holy. It is the life that comes from recovering what's been lost, uncovering what is hidden, and learning to hope in what is small.

Lost, hidden, and small—for many Christians, this is what we want to be saved *from*. They are the last words we'd choose to describe the kingdom of God. They surprise and offend us, but they shouldn't. Jesus couldn't have been clearer in warning us not to expect his realm to resemble the empires humans create. He told his followers that his kingdom was like a lost coin, a lost sheep, a lost son. He explained that the kingdom was in the midst of them and also that it was hidden, like a priceless pearl buried in a field. He warned them that, once they found it, they'd have to sell everything they had to attain it. He revealed that holiness was contagious, that it would appear small, even despised—like a mustard seed or corrupting yeast—but its power would unexpectedly and inexorably transform reality.

* * *

In a long wilderness season of futility and failure, I found the salvation I wasn't looking for. I began to realize that the way of salvation begins with restored sight. As I began to accept my own limitedness, a wild peace began to invade my life. I'd long cultivated a serious, sophisticated, deep theological persona, but in my helplessness, I could no longer sustain it. Gradually, I unclenched into a childlike, wonder-filled trust in a goodness I cannot command or explain. A goodness that is near me, in me, around me, but not of me. A goodness that does not answer to me. I don't have to be like God anymore. All of this has astonished and liberated me.

I'll confess that some days I resent knowing it. Old desires die hard. It takes a long time to retrain your spiritual palate to delight and savor in what is lost, hidden, and small. These were the last places I sought abundance. But if everything beautiful isn't, then the opposite is also true. Sometimes what seems like loss is a gift. Sometimes what seems undesirable is the only thing that satisfies. Sometimes what looks as if it will destroy you ends up being what saves you.

Sometimes what is lost, what is hidden, and what is small is sacred.

Let me tell you the story of another invasive species that flourishes in a non-native land. A tree grows in Brooklyn and across New York City. Yes, it is *that* tree, the one from Betty Smith's story. Its scientific name is *Ailanthus altissima*, but it is commonly known as the tree of heaven. People say it came to be called that because it grows fast, straight and narrow, and toward the sky. But I think the name is apt because of its propensity to grow in derelict spaces, amid broken concrete, in nutritionally depleted soil. The tree of heaven restores creation. Literally. It cleanses the air, makes oxygen, and provides shade and shelter. It does much more than lift the eye toward the sky; it makes life lush and verdant here and now on the ground.

Like the lanternfly, the tree of heaven is not indigenous to this land. Like the lanternfly, its presence also transforms its environment. But unlike the lanternfly, it does not bring destruction. It displaces everything in its surrounding environment, yes. But the environment it invades is blight. It brings regeneration, it brings growth and breath into nature-forsaken places. Like the kingdom of God, the tree of heaven restores flourishing. Lanternflies bring death into living spaces. Trees of heaven restore life to barren ones.

Jesus knew it would be hard for us to recognize the kingdom of God, so he gave us parables: sacred stories to act as maps to help us navigate the distance between what is and what appears to be. He gave us stories about lost people being found, hidden treasure being uncovered, and small and weak things with the power to heal and transform. Pastors like me preach and teach those parables, but we often stop short of practicing them. Christians may know these verses, but we don't often live them—until God graciously opens our eyes to the destructive power of false beauty that blinds us to the good and real. Until the paths to power and excellence and control are graciously destroyed. Until what is lost, hidden, and small is all that is left to us, and so we are forced to perceive them. Then we recover our sight. Then we come alive.

This is the story of how we learn to see in the kingdom of God.

This is the story of the way I came alive.

This is the story of the community that came alive alongside and around me.

This is the story of the beautiful life that isn't and of the beautiful life that is.

Part I

LOST

Finding Ourselves in Christ

1

WE ARE THE LOST ONES

MY YOUNGEST DAUGHTER was three and a half when the pandemic shut the world down. We pulled her out of preschool, and as a working mother I was grateful to enroll her in the hastily chartered Big Sisters Academy. In the rare moments that the abstract terror of COVID-19 subsided, I cherished sitting around the dining room table with all three of my girls. None of us produced our best work, but there was something magical in the thirty-second intervals we were able to do our separate work together. When I wasn't busy hating it, part of me loved that, for this tenuous season, our family of five didn't split off in five different directions five days a week. We created a ritual of morning meetings where we took turns saying a prayer and sharing a Bible verse and intention for the day. It was sweetly woo-woo, and we practiced it for exactly one week. I knew I wasn't called or equipped to homeschool, but there were moments I recognized that, in the context of the horror, this togetherness was a gift. Or could be, if I could just dig a little deeper and get myself together. I lived in self-flagellating hope.

And then six months in, I heard the littlest one singing the alphabet song and realized she had lost the last twelve letters. She'd sing her way to the letter *p* and then unironically declare, "Now I know my ABC's, next time won't you sing with me?" I took a deep breath, admired her singing and then began to explain in my gentlest, crunchy-granola, this-is-a-gift, homeschooling, mama voice that she'd left some letters out. She assured me that she had not. The more I tried to tell her, the more indignant she became.

I reminded her that her sister's name begins with a *q* and that letter was missing in her song. She was unconvinced. I tried singing with her to steer her back on track. Nevertheless, she persisted. She was so proud and certain. She was sure she'd learned her letters a long time ago. She was insulted and threatened by the suggestion that she had lost an essential part of the song. Her identity was at stake. She was a big girl who knew her letters, not a baby still learning them. She wasn't interested in additional letters. She was sticking with the song she knew how to sing.

The church is two thousand years old. In the context of human history, the church is a preschooler—one who has forgotten indispensable parts of our foundational Christ song. But we are outraged when anyone tries to help us recover the essential missing pieces. This is *our* song, after all. The one we've been given to share with the world. Our identity is at stake. How can we be who we are called to be if we don't know what we are called to share? How can we claim to love Jesus and also admit that we don't fully know him? And yet, how can we deny it when the gap between the Jesus we meet in Scriptures and the majority of North American churches claiming his name is an ever-widening chasm?

In the Gospels, Jesus is infamous for welcoming sinners, surrendering advantages, embracing outcasts, challenging the religious establishment, provoking the powerful, rejecting acclaim, and centering the very ones the world pushes to the margins. In contemporary American culture, the church of Jesus Christ is infamous for sex scandals, persecuting the vulnerable, pursuing political power, insularity, mega-institutions, wealth, elitism, pride, violence, bigotry, and culture wars. The song we insist on singing to the world is not the one we were given to sing.

Still, the whole song is there, waiting to be recovered. To learn it again requires that we surrender our self-determined expert status. This relearning is the kind of ego death that births new life. I believe this relearning is what Jesus means when he tells his friends that anyone who enters the kingdom of God must come as a little child. Paradoxically, the only way to become mature is to recognize that you are not. We are not holy experts. We were never meant to be spiritual authorities or the source of truth. We are spiritual children, preschoolers who have lost foundational pieces of our faith and understanding. We are forever loved and chosen, but until we recover the whole Jesus song, we cannot follow the Lord faithfully. Until we recover the whole song, our loud faith in the One who saves us is idolatrous, and we worship a copy of a copy of a copy of Jesus. We pound the sacred truths of Christ we manage to remember into a golden calf mascot for our flailing, faltering, dangerous institutions. We are formed by the culture of America instead of the culture of the kingdom of God.

What we have lost makes us the lost.

* * *

Growing up on the edges of Christian communities, I heard a lot about "the lost." I spent more years than I care to admit quietly terrified that no matter how often I prayed or how fervently I worshiped, I was one of them. As a concession to my grandfather, I was "illegally" baptized as an infant, but I wasn't raised in the church. When my parents returned to their hometown to begin raising a family, they decided not to join a country club or a church because both were segregated. My mother began to sporadically take us to Sunday School when I was in late elementary school after realizing that none of us knew the Lord's Prayer. But the intent was to give us cultural competency, not faith.

I loved church. It felt like home. But it also felt like I was always separated from everyone else by a thin piece of glass. In some way I felt but could not understand, I had a kind of probationary status. I might belong but that remained to be seen, someday and by someone other than me. No one talked about the lost in the upper-middle-class Presbyterian church of my childhood, but if they were the people who didn't quite belong, I suspected I was one of them.

And then in high school, my suspicions were confirmed. I fell in love with a charismatic Christian boy, and on dates we sneaked away to worship with his nondenominational Pentecostal community. I learned there that I wasn't a Christian because I was part of the "frozen chosen" and that no church I'd ever previously belonged to was actually a church at all. I sat on the edges of fiery worship services, listened to prophecies, and watched as folks caught the Holy Spirit and ran exuberantly around the room. I kept a tin box full of teaching tapes in my car to play as I drove up and down Kentucky hills. I met apostles, heard people give testimonies of healings and exorcisms, tried to speak in tongues, and was informed repeatedly that, in spite of all of this, I was *not* a Christian.

For reasons not clearly articulated at the time, but which I now recognize as a savage strand of predestination, I was one of the lost. There was nothing anyone could do about it, least of all me. Each of my boyfriend's siblings separately took me aside and asked me to stop dating him. They were afraid that my lost status would corrupt their brother's holiness and jeopardize his eternal salvation.

As an adult, I'm deeply aware that the way a child experiences Christian community is a factor of many things and rarely reflects the intentions of community members. And as a pastor, I'm ruefully aware of the gap between intentions and impact. I'm not casting judgment on any of the churches who welcomed me in as a kid; I'm only sharing these stories to show that, while its expressions are varied, there is an almost universal understanding of the lost as members of an out-group. Across the theological spectrum, lostness is understood as the intrinsic quality of people who do not belong in Christian communities. Some communities teach that the lost are to be feared and shunned, others that the lost are to be welcomed and indoctrinated. Some teach about lostness explicitly, others implicitly, but almost all teach that the biblical concept of the lost refers to *people who are not us*. The mainline church has a benign indifference to lost people, the Pentecostal church sees them as a threat, but both communities understand the lost as individuals and outsiders.

* * *

This is not the way Jesus talked about the lost. In Luke 15, Jesus tells three parables about lostness. "Suppose one of you has a hundred sheep and loses one of them," he says. "Or suppose a woman has ten silver coins and loses one," Jesus adds. "There was a man who had two sons," Jesus continues, with a third story. "The younger one said to his father, 'Father, give me my share of the estate.'"

Jesus tells these three stories while surrounded by two crowds of people. The crowd closest to him was made up of people who were unwelcome in the local faith community. Jesus attracts a crowd, but it's the wrong crowd. Luke identifies them as tax collectors and sinners. We tend to simplify the story to make it more comfortable. We imagine that everyone in the crowd was unfairly perceived as sinful by self-righteous bigots. And maybe some were hookers with hearts of gold. But the tax collectors crowding around Jesus enriched themselves by extorting excess fees from an already destitute people. The greed of the tax collectors meant that families lost ancestral land, were often reduced to begging, and sometimes watched beloved children starve. People were being taxed to death. What the tax collectors did was brutal, lethal, and legal. And yet there the tax collectors were—human cogs in the bureaucratic death machine—listening to Jesus.

There was a second crowd near Jesus that day, keeping distance from the first. Luke tells us the faith leaders and Scripture experts in that second crowd were horrified by the people Jesus welcomed and shared meals with. We need to understand that we would have been offended and confused as well. Jesus sees that people are more than the very worst things they've ever done. That's a beautiful and liberating truth—until the worst thing a person has ever done is done to you. Then grace becomes a stumbling block.

Years ago, my family got the paper delivered to our house. In the mornings, I'd often sit and read it at the table while my kids slurped their cereal. One day I was looking at a story with the headline "Father Forgives Murderer of His Child." My middle daughter was in first grade at the time, and I forgot that meant she could actually read. She looked up at me with a horrified expression and said, "You would never do that would you, Mommy? You would never forgive someone if they killed me, would you?" Reflected in seven-year-old eyes, a theology of grace was betrayal. I stammered that I couldn't imagine it, wouldn't want to, but that I believed Jesus would want me to and would help me if I asked him. She was deeply confused and hurt by my answer.

It's easy to feel self-righteous about the self-righteousness of the Pharisees and teachers who condemned Jesus's welcoming table if you take it upon yourself to release the tension from the story. If you tell the story so that the people around Jesus that day were only guilty of loving the wrong people, or not memorizing enough Scripture verses, or losing their library books, if you rewrite history and cast the tax collectors as overworked and underappreciated public servants, if you decide that everyone around Jesus that day was simply a victim of prejudice and misunderstanding—well, then Luke is telling a simple and boring story.

But if you don't numb yourself to the cries of those who were oppressed, if you have scars from hurt people hurting people, or if you have ever suffered or caused suffering: Then you know that sometimes to label someone a sinner is not slander, but fact. If you know the ways systems can commodify and destroy the most vulnerable lives, then you understand that to be a tax collector in first-century Palestine was as morally charged as being an SS officer in Germany in the 1940s, a plantation owner in the antebellum United States, or one of the Homeland Security agents who pried sobbing children out of the arms of their parents at the US-Mexico border.

So Jesus was surrounded by a crowd of sinners and tax collectors. And *that* crowd was surrounded by a second crowd of faith leaders and experts. And everyone in each crowd was aware of the sins of the people in the other. And in response to the sin and brokenness of both crowds, Jesus told three stories about lostness.

When Jesus talked about the lost, he was talking to bitterly divided groups of people. He told them stories about a sheep, a coin, and a son. Jesus didn't talk about the lost the way we do. He didn't tell stories about an out-group who are intrinsically other and must be transformed before they can belong. He told stories about a valuable resource in danger, about a precious object gone missing, and about a beloved one who has walked away. He told stories about essential things, things that must be recovered so that the community can be healed and restored.

The parable of the lost sheep is the story of a part separated from the whole in a way that endangers the entire community. The parable of the missing coin is a story in which the loss of something valuable brings a person's character and survival into question. The parable of the prodigal son is the story of a family whose broken relationships threaten not just the present but the future of their whole community.

In each story, what is missing threatens the identity of what is still present. How can you be a shepherd if you allow a sheep to wander away without mounting a recovery operation? How can you be a responsible steward if you lose one-tenth of all you have? How can you call yourself a loving father if you don't scan the horizon each day, hoping for the chance to run and welcome your child home? In Jesus's stories, what is lost is precious and must be recovered.

And in Jesus's stories, what is lost belongs. Even in their absence, the lost remain intrinsically part of the whole. The lost sheep still belongs to the flock. The lost coin is still the property of the woman. The younger son is ever and always the child of the father, no matter how far he wanders or what he does while he is gone.

And when Jesus tells stories about the lost, their absence is not negligible. Nothing is better without them. The discovery that a sheep has gone missing is a crisis. The revelation that the tenth coin is not in the bag is a catastrophe. The younger son's decision to leave creates a devastating hole. No one in Jesus's stories is able to move on while what has been lost remains unfound. In all three stories, recovery of the lost is cause for immediate and exuberant celebration.

And in all three stories, normalcy is suspended when the lost go missing. Life enters a sort of limbo until what is lost has been recovered. Work cannot go on. Progress cannot be made. Celebrations are postponed. The recovery process is risky, disruptive, and even shameful. Nevertheless, it must be attempted.

So we can continue to talk about the lost as people who don't belong or as people whose absence is irrelevant, if we want to. But such talk just betrays how unfamiliar and uninterested we are in our own sacred texts. Jesus tells stories of lostness to two crowds bitterly divided from one another. He says that wholeness and health are an illusion until what has been lost is found and wholeness is recovered and celebrated.

* * *

It is not new news that Christian communities in North America are withering on the vine. There is no shortage of voices ready to tell us who is to blame for that. The answer is always different iterations of the same root cause. It's the people over there who are ruining it for the rest of us. One crowd is always pointing fingers at the other. But I think the truth is simpler and more devastating.

We are the problem. Like my daughter and her fourteen-letter alphabet, we have lost essential pieces of the Christian way, but we are confident in the rightness of our faith, committed to what we have, and threatened by anything unfamiliar. We are certain that if other people would just get it right and be like us, everything would be fine. And any messenger who comes suggesting that we might be the problem better be wearing Teflon underwear, because they can go straight to hell. I know because I tried to send a few of them there.

In December 2008, I accepted my first call as a solo pastor serving a beautiful urban church in east Charlotte. After four years of graduate school and another eight years as an associate pastor, I was ready. I couldn't wait to avoid the mistakes every other pastor has ever made. I was eager to creatively serve our neighbors. I was committed to humbly loving members of the church. I was ready to work harder than anyone had ever worked. The congregation I served had been losing members for decades. I wouldn't have admitted it, but I was sure that once I got started and won everyone over, we'd grow like a weed. I was an adorable idiot.

Fast-forward two-and-a-half years later. I'd launched a half dozen creative neighborhood ministries. I authentically loved the people in the church and cheerfully worked about seventy-five hours a week. I couldn't see it (and wouldn't have thought it mattered if I had), but I was a trainwreck. What I *could* see was that the church was not growing. At all. We had a summer camp, an after-school program, an arts ministry, and a meal distribution program. Each year we hosted two major neighborhood festivals and sponsored nine Girl Scout troops.

But nobody new wanted to worship with us on Sunday mornings. And honestly, if we hadn't been hemorrhaging money, I'd have accepted that as inevitable and carried on. But each month's budget report revealed that carrying on was not an option. In desperation, we enrolled ourselves in the church transformation program sponsored by our denomination. But I was there to be praised and resourced. I was not there for spiritual enlightenment, because I did not think I required any. I was happy singing my faith song. I knew I already knew everything I needed to know. Nobody needed to tell me anything. I was—ahem—a pastor.

I was also a fool. Over the next months, God gave me a spiritual crisis, one that forced me to make a decision. Did I want to be validated, or did I want to be changed? Did I want to keep singing the song I knew how to sing until the bitter end and pointing fingers at other people who were doing wrong? Or did I want to adopt a posture of humility and learn what I was sure I didn't need to know? Did I want to be right, or did I want to be faithful?

I could keep doing what I knew to do as hard as I could for as long as I could and call it success (or a failure that was someone else's fault). Or I could listen when someone loved me and my church enough to tell me that I had lost some precious and irreplaceable pieces of the Jesus revelation. I could listen when someone told me that I wasn't responsible for anyone else's faithfulness, but I was responsible for my own. I could listen when someone told me that the work of recovery was mine to do.

The words of Jesus have a way of getting under your skin. In the Sermon on the Mount, he warns his followers against the spiritual trap of judgment: "Why do you look at the speck of sawdust in your brother's eye and pay no attention to the plank in your own eye?" (Matt 7:3). I've preached that sermon a dozen times, quoted that quote several dozen more, sucked my teeth over it plenty, but I always read it as if it were about other people. "Why are you so judgmental, you Wrong Kind of Christian? Don't you know that Jesus said not to criticize the speck in your brother's eye while ignoring the log in your own?"

When I finally stopped numbing myself and avoiding the crisis by overworking, when I finally began to face the reality that this congregation I served was inexorably dying, when I finally began to seek the source of the problem—at first all I could see were the specks in other people's eyes. Why did our neighbors want to send their kids to our after-school program but not worship with us? Why did the college students want to volunteer with us but not worship with us? Why did people want to go to brunch but not worship with us? Why did the people who did want to worship on Sundays want to go to megachurches with smoke machines and not worship with us? Why did the denomination discontinue the grant program we would have qualified for? Why didn't the church members invite their friends? Why didn't people want to join a church with a female pastor? Why didn't people of color want to join a historically and predominantly white church? (They'd see that we were ready to welcome them if they would only come to worship with us!) Why couldn't everyone else in the world see that who I was and what I did had worth and validate me by coming to worship with us? Why did Jesus call me into ministry and then make me a failure?

I *knew* I was faithful. What I couldn't understand was why no one else managed to be. Why, I bitterly wondered, was Jesus not sending anyone to help me help him? I saw everyone else as varying degrees of the problem. I saw myself as the solution. I didn't see the Lord at all. I wasn't looking for him.

Help showed up in disguise, as it so often does. In this case it was in the person of a perfectly coiffed Southern Baptist pastor.

When he was assigned to be our church transformation coach, the Southern Baptist pastor generously agreed to disagree with me on the question of women's ordination. I sure could see plenty of crap in his eye.

But I could also see that the churches he served grew. I deeply resented having to learn anything from him, but I knew he knew things that I didn't know and had done things I hadn't been able to do. I didn't believe he had anything to teach me, but I wasn't going to allow my bitterness to risk the future of the congregation.

Here was a man who didn't properly see and value me, and he was just plain wrong about so much. There was so much of the core of Christianity I felt he didn't understand, so much of the song he had never learned to sing. I was offended that Jesus would even associate with him, much less anoint and bless his ministry, much less make him my teacher. At first, I was so full of resentment, so busy reassuring myself that I was the truly faithful one, so busy keeping score of how much and how wrong he was, that I didn't bother seeing or hearing him at all.

It took me a long time to recognize myself as part of the angry judgmental crowd criticizing Jesus, indignant over who he talked with and ate with and included. It took me a long time to understand that someone else being wrong about something didn't equate to my being right about everything. It took me a very long time to accept that I, too, was singing the Jesus song loudly and confidently but only in part.

It turns out I wasn't the only one being judged; I was also the one judging. I wasn't only the one with powerful spiritual truth to share; I was also one who desperately needed revelation. I wasn't only a pastor with a ministry to practice; I also needed to be ministered to. I wasn't only a pastor with so much to share with my community; I was also a woman in spiritual crisis, desperately in need of wisdom that could only come from my community and healing that I could only receive from God.

With the clarity of hindsight, I can now see how much I was like my daughter in that season. Faced with problems I could not solve and needs I could not fill, my instinct was to do what I knew how to do but harder, faster, and louder. I sang the song I knew to sing, certain that if people would just listen to me, everything would be fine. I was the preacher of a faith I did not know how to practice. I knew how to talk about Jesus, how to serve and minister for Jesus, but not how to seek in him the pieces that were missing in me. And that's mainly because I never slowed down enough to notice there were pieces missing in me.

It wasn't a longing for new revelation or a desire for greater intimacy that compelled me to search for something more. It was simply that I couldn't go on any more the way I was. I couldn't run fast enough to get away from the truth that my life and my faith were falling apart and I couldn't hold either together any longer. I couldn't deny any longer that when I thought of Jesus, I wasn't filled with love and trust and hope but hurt and resentment and anger. Maybe you are hiding similar pain you "aren't supposed to feel" not only from others but also from yourself.

You don't have to be a pastor to be afraid to acknowledge that your faith is hurting you, afraid that if you seek healing you might find relief but at the high cost of the community you love and even your own soul. I was afraid that if I acknowledged, even to myself, the ways my faith in Jesus wasn't bringing me anything resembling abundant life anymore, I would lose the only solace that remained to me. So I numbed my pain and silenced my doubts with certainty.

It took me a long time to recognize that all my questions and confusion and bitterness—all those losses and setbacks and failures—were not punishment or judgment but a profound spiritual gift called disorientation. They were the searingly bright light that finally helped me to see what I was missing.

Maybe your pain is a searchlight too.

* * *

So Jesus told three parables about lostness. He told those stories surrounded by two crowds of people, each consumed by hating the other. One crowd knew they were sinners; the other believed they were righteous. One crowd was seeking forgiveness and salvation; the other believed both were theirs to distribute or withhold. One crowd was desperate for a new life; the other was desperate to hold on to the life they had. Both crowds were full of beloved people missing essential pieces. Both had lost vital parts of themselves and so were unable to live as they were created to live. Both crowds had become the lost.

But the stories Jesus told weren't about the people in either crowd; they were stories about life in the kingdom of God. In Jesus's stories, *lost* isn't a word used to label people who are unlike us. *Lost* is the word we use to describe the irreplaceable and incalculable that is missing in our lives.

When Jesus tells his stories, he doesn't seem to be very interested in why something was lost or whose fault the lostness is. He's encouraging people that what has been lost can be recovered. He's telling us it's worth the effort to seek. People who listen deeply to Jesus's stories about lostness stop asking the question "What's wrong with *them*?" They begin to wonder what essential pieces of their faith and life might be missing—and what it would look like to stop long enough to begin seeking.

If you want to find something you've lost, first you have to recognize that something is missing. Jesus told stories about lostness to people who couldn't imagine what wholeness might be like. It's so easy for us as people of faith to spend our lives focused on the faults and sins and missing pieces of other people. We may not even be wrong in our assessment. Still, we won't recover wholeness in Christ that way. Jesus says there is more rejoicing in the kingdom of God when we recover what is lost than when we hold on to what we've kept. Jesus's parables about lostness teach us that the path into the kingdom of God requires loosening our grip on what we have so that we can be open to what else God might have to give to us. It requires us to stop singing what we know for long enough to listen for what we've forgotten.

In the following three chapters, I'll share pieces of the kingdom of God that my community recovered in our long, fruitful season of disorientation. Shalom, kinship, and trinity were not unfamiliar to me as concepts, but I knew them as abstract, future-oriented ideals. Yet I now believe them to be essential aspects of the culture of the kingdom of God here and now. If you'd asked me whether my church was trying to live out our understanding of shalom or kinship (let alone trinity!), I would have rolled my eyes to cover up how threatened I was by your question. I could preach passionately and teach competently about all three. I had passed my ordination exams and recognized them as ontologically true; Wasn't that enough? If you pressed me, I would have argued that shalom, kinship, and trinity were things we talked about and longed for on this side of eternity but that we could only experience on the other. And if you quoted to me Jesus's teaching from Luke 17:21 that "the kingdom of God is in your midst," I would have faked a pastoral emergency and left the room.

Since I knew what shalom, kinship, and trinity were, it didn't occur to me that our community had lost them. I was satisfied with the church as a repository for inert theological concepts, and I didn't yet have even the capacity to desire to live what I knew was true. Like many other American Christians, I inherited a faith that had lost these three things without even an awareness of their absence.

In our risky and costly search for wholeness, we discovered that we find the kingdom of God when we commit to the messy, imperfect, inefficient, and foolish attempt to live as if we believed that Jesus was telling us the truth when he revealed that the kingdom of God is already in the midst of us, and that when we seek, we will find.

2

SHALOM

We All Fare Well

I WENT TO many protests in the summer of 2020. For that one season, it seemed as if the country, after seeing law enforcement officer Derek Chauvin execute George Floyd in broad daylight, was finally going to demand due process and equal protection under the law for Black Americans. Seemed like that to white people anyway. Always masked and distanced, I sometimes went during the day with our family, my older daughters carrying homemade signs and my husband pushing our youngest in the stroller. Other times I went alone at night, wearing my clergy robes and stole, hoping my privileged presence would protect the people around me. As a disciple of Jesus, I knew I could not follow him without walking in these protests. As a white woman serving a multiethnic church, I knew it was important that Black and white members of my congregation not only heard me preach justice on Sundays but saw me in the crowd, following Black organizers and people of color the other days of the week.

Although I serve as a leader in my church, I knew my role in these protests was not to lead but to follow. So I wore what organizers asked me to wear, stood where they told me to stand, knelt when they asked me to kneel, raised a clenched fist and held silence when they called for it. And when it was time to chant, I chanted. The names of the dead, mostly, a never-ending list of Black people murdered by the state, and slogans: "Black Lives Matter," "It Ends Now," "Tell Me What Democracy Looks Like; This Is What Democracy Looks Like," "Say His Name," "Say Her Name," "Say Their Names." It was a worship liturgy as pure and powerful and prayerful as I've ever known.

There was one chant, perhaps the most popular one, that I did not understand: "No Justice, No Peace." I said it anyway but with deep discomfort. No justice, no peace. It sounded like a threat in my white ears. No justice—now that much was clear to me. There is no justice in a system where unarmed citizens are executed by officers of the state without cause or repercussions.

But the "No Peace" part of the chant scared me. It sounded like we were making a threat. I thought the phrase meant that since there is no justice, we will make sure there is no peace. Since there is no justice, we will disrupt and destroy the peace. Sure, I knew these were nonviolent protests. I knew the organizers were committed to nonviolence, and I knew protesters were in danger from the police but did not pose danger to law enforcement officers or anyone else. Still, I choked a little on those words. It didn't feel right to say them. But it felt more wrong to keep silent, or to substitute my comfort for the wisdom of the leaders. So I leaned not on my own understanding and spoke the words I did not understand.

In that summer of fear and grief and rage, I shouted the words while quietly turning them over and over again in my mind, pondering them in my heart—until one day, the meaning became suddenly, blindingly clear.

I did not understand the chant because I did not understand all the words. Literally, I did not know peace.

* * *

Author and writing coach Jonathan Rogers has a delightful essay on *mondegreens*: misheard words in a phrase that leads to a radical misunderstanding. The term was created in the 1950s by author Sylvia Wright to describe her misunderstanding of a Scottish ballad her mother used to sing. Sylvia's mother sang her a haunting folk song depicting the murder of the Earl of Moray and his wife, Lady "Mondegreen." Years later, she read the lyrics and was astonished to find the song depicted only one death, the earl's. But the lyrics did describe how, after the earl died, they "laid him on the green." Lady Mondegreen didn't die in the song—because she never existed. So when a father introduces his young son to the concept "knowledge is power" and immediately ascribes the quote to the philosopher Francis Bacon, the boy, unfamiliar with sixteenth century English philosophers, hears not a name but the confusing phrase "France is bacon." For years, when he asks his teachers to clarify, they wax poetic on the power of knowledge but confoundingly refuse to explain how wisdom transforms the nation of France into nonkosher cured meat. Finally, he sees it in writing and the penny drops: Francis Bacon, not France is bacon.

We all have embarrassing stories about misheard lyrics or childish misunderstandings of colloquialisms or metaphors. Rogers, who is also a professor, relates his consternation in grading a college student's final essay on "Donkey Oatey"—a mondegreen that instantly and devastatingly revealed she'd never opened the book *Don Quixote*. Mondegreens are funny when they're a misheard lyric to a pop song but catastrophic when it leads students to believe that great works of literature feature noble but doomed talking donkeys.

But as Rogers points out in his essay, even after we identify mondegreens as false, we remain influenced by them. Admit it: You still hear "Rock the cash bar," "Excuse me while I kiss this guy," and "Blame it on Lorraine." Personally, I'll always sing about Taylor Swift's long list of "Starbucks lovers." These foundational misunderstandings don't vanish, even when we discover they are laughably false; as Rogers points out, "the mind calcifies around its initial idea."

For me, *peace* will always be a theological and philosophical mondegreen, a concept I initially misunderstood. It's a foundational misunderstanding I will always have to consciously unlearn and relearn. Growing up in safety and privilege, I never thought much about peace. I was a fish, and it was the water I was swimming in. Peace was a void word, an empty container, that only communicated the absence of its opposite.

As a child, I believed that peace was the absence of war and dangerous violence. In the absence of conflict (or the absence of awareness of it), peace was the default. As I grew into adolescence, peace became an emotional state expected from me: the absence of pain and passion and intense emotions. Peace meant staying calm and quiet, maintaining order, avoiding chaos. Those seeking peace went to yoga classes, studied Zen philosophy, and chanted mantras.

Then when I started to become a Christian, I learned that the best and purest peace was spiritual peace, which was inner peace that came from loving Jesus correctly. Inner peace could be achieved by transcending worldly concerns and convictions. Peace meant not really caring—but in a spiritualized and admirable way. Jesus talked about peace, but I wasn't interested in those passages of Scripture. I liked the stuff Jesus *did*, feeding and healing and flipping tables. It never occurred to me that the latter was the manifestation of the former.

I pictured peace as the realm where white angels on fluffy white clouds in white robes played harps and pan flutes. Nice, I guess, but detached from reality, unattainable and, frankly, boring. This is a Donkey Oatey-level self-own. My tepid, sterile, disembodied conceptualization of peace reveals just how much my moral imagination was formed by my culture and not by Scripture.

If peace is confidence in or calm resignation to the status quo, then crowds of people chanting "No Justice, No Peace" are not only making threats but fulfilling them by their very existence. But if we actually open the book we call the Bible, we won't find anything like that concept of peace there.

* * *

The word most often translated as "peace" in Scripture is the Hebrew word *shalom*. It is shalom in Genesis when the spirit of God moves across the darkness and void, calling forth life and light, stars and clouds, mountains, valleys, caverns and caves, oceans and deserts all teeming with life. It is shalom in the garden, when the first humans lived in wholeness and freedom, together with God and one another, sharing sacred communion as they labored in paradise and walked and talked face to face in the cool of the evening. In the Garden of Eden, the beloved ones knew the sacred rhythms of work and rest, and they received and delighted in the goodness of all God set before them. And from the beginning, shalom included the goodness of limit: "You shall not eat of the tree of the knowledge of good and evil" (Gen 2:17; my translation). There is a holy kind of flourishing in accepting that some things are set apart.

And then shalom was shattered. The first humans took what was not theirs to take, centered their own desires, and disregarded divine wisdom. As a result, death, enmity, and violence entered into reality. God's response to destruction is never more destruction. God's response is ever and always shalom: tenderness and repair; reconciliation and re-creation; a steadfast, loving kindness present in the chaos and disorder.

The part of the fall we never talk about is God's response of shalom. Seeing the humans' shame at their nakedness, God sits down in a corner of the garden and sews them garments.

Shalom is the triumph of God. God's response to the fall is a promise to reestablish shalom. God declares that the powers of hate and harm unleashed and embodied by the snake will not ultimately claim creation. God promises they will be crushed by the Son of Man, who will be known as the Prince of shalom. He is the son of the woman who will crush the head of the serpent. He is the One who destroys destruction. Mondegreen peace might be a faux, Zen acceptance: "It is what it is." But shalom? That's something entirely different: active restoration of all that shouldn't be into its original intrinsic wholeness and goodness.

There's a delightfully strange line in the apostle Paul's letter to the church in Rome that only makes sense if you know authentic shalom. Closing his letter with words of empowerment for a suffering and beleaguered community, Paul encourages them to carry on bravely in the way of Jesus, confidently resisting evil because "the God of peace [shalom] will soon crush Satan under your feet" (Rom 16:20). Far from accepting evil as inevitable or seeking ways of coping with or avoiding it, shalom anticipates and participates in overcoming evil with goodness and love. Shalom never means the protection of a few from pain and destruction. Shalom is the holy restored to the whole, the glory of God once again covering the whole earth.

When we walk in the streets chanting "No Justice, No Peace," we are an apocalypse, an "uncovering"—a revealing what already is. Some live on safe streets, some learn in fine schools, some receive excellent medical care, and some find justice in the court. But until these things are true for all, there is no shalom. Until then, there is no real peace, only a powerfully seductive false peace that lures us with promises of comfort and personal safety in exchange for the precious lives of our siblings. Once again, we sell our sacred birthright for a mess of porridge.

The simple Bible stories you may have learned in Sunday school have much to show us about true and false peace, if we let them. They've been planted in our hard hearts all along, waiting to take root and bear holy fruit. The book of Exodus is the story of God liberating the Hebrew people from slavery in Egypt. The Egyptian empire was a realm of false peace. The elite had power and wielded it with such precision that the few could control and literally own the many, making it legal for the heads of infants to be crushed at birth and illegal to protect new life, making it safe to kill an infant and dangerous to nourish one. If we believe that peace exists wherever the powerful feel safe and secure, no matter who is hurt and hurting, then Pharaoh was the true "prince of peace." After all, he only acted against the Hebrew people because they were a threat to his safety and power. He only acted to preserve law and order.

If peace is achieved through the affluence and control of the powerful few, then when Pharaoh enslaved the Hebrew people and weakened them by requiring them to make bricks without straw, he was making peace. If peace is simply the absence of chaos and the presence of order and control, then Pharaoh was the prince of peace when he ordered the infanticide of Hebrew babies. If peace exists everywhere as long as there is tranquility somewhere, then it was God Almighty and Moses the redeemer who disturbed the peace when they went into Pharaoh's courtroom and demanded the liberation of the oppressed. Releasing the captives would have required reordering society, practically and morally. How can we afford to build our projects if we have to pay for labor? How can we allow the people whose children we killed to live freely among us? How would we ever feel righteous or safe in our homes then?

Civilization, as everyone knew it, depended on maintaining a brutal social hierarchy. Liberating captives and ending the suffering of those with no power would have disrupted everyone's lives. Liberation would have derailed the progress of civilization. So Pharaoh chose to preserve the false peace and maintain the status quo. He refused Moses's ridiculous request. But a false peace, manufactured by oppression, can lead to sacred chaos, in this case ten plagues of destruction. Moses, the great liberator and emancipator, was a man of true shalom, and his work created chaos, confusion, and painful change.

No one living in Egypt knew they were characters in a biblical story. They were all people just trying to survive the world they'd inherited. Those who were suffering and oppressed would have experienced Moses as an answer to prayer and a deliverer of freedom. Those who were comfortable because of or despite the suffering of their neighbors would have experienced Moses as a terrorist. Depending on how you understood peace, he was either bringing it or destroying it.

There is a kind of false peace manufactured by the mighty out of the misery of the majority. But that kind of peace is a diabolical mondegreen of shalom. Shalom disrupts deadly order and control, crushes oppression and unleashes the chaos of liberation, reconciliation and new life.

The more I read the story of Exodus, the more it troubles me. I'm grateful for the sacred discomfort it gives me. Recently I noticed a line in the text I'd never seen before. After all the negotiations, all the lies, all the plagues, all the resistance, and after the tenth plague of death passed over the land of Egypt and the powerful finally felt the pain of the false peace they'd perpetuated against the powerless: After all of that deadly denial, in Exodus 12 God tells Moses that it is finally time for the enslaved Hebrews to leave. And the people gather all their stuff and leave in such a hurry they cannot add yeast to their bread. Upon the Lord's command, they have asked for and received reparations from their neighbors. Now they herd all their cattle and livestock and stream out of the cities destroyed by greed and grief.

But they do not go alone. Exodus 12:37 tells us about 600,000 Hebrew men, not counting women or children (because no one bothered to count them) escaped to freedom. And somehow I never noticed the next line. Exodus 12:38 reads: "Many other people also went up with them, and also droves of livestock, flocks and herds."

"Many other people" also went out with the Hebrews. Wait. Who were they? Scholars argue over these folks who joined the caravan. The Message translation calls them "a crowd of riff-raff tagging along." The New King James Bible names them "a mixed multitude."

What I see here is a path for me—an invitation to be part of that mixed multitude who long for the freedom of their neighbors because they understand that it is their own freedom as well.

I want to be part of the riffraff who get in line and follow the liberation caravan into an unknown future, even if it means that those who still put their trust in the crumbling empire see me as a traitor or a fool. There is more abundance living on the edge of a community of shalom than in the center of a society constructed on false peace.

* * *

The promises of shalom are not promises of a new and unfamiliar life but the sacred return to the old life—the first life of new creation. We often translate *shalom* as "peace," but a better English word is actually "welfare": a place or realm or culture where all fare well. "Come, you who have no money, buy bread and eat," reads the prophet's invitation (Isa 55:1; my translation). When the prophets speak of shalom, we dismiss it as crazy talk. But shalom, true peace, bears almost no resemblance to the shallow peace that satisfies us in a world defined by destruction and despair. We cannot imagine an economy built on abundance and generosity. So Scripture describes how it will be: In the kingdom of God, citizens "beat their swords into plowshares, and their spears into pruning hooks" because when we have shalom, the tools we designed to protect ourselves and control our neighbors become obsolete. So we repurpose them into instruments of growth and nourishment (Isa 2:11). "Everyone shall live in their own house and sit under the shade of their own vine, and no one shall make them afraid," says the prophet Micah (Mic 4:4; my translation). The peasant farmer will no longer be oppressed by the merchants of war. There will no longer be any reason for riot or revolt. This is not a peace a human government can achieve or impose from the top down. This is a kind of peace we can only cocreate with our neighbors. Shalom grows from the bottom up. Without God, it is impossible—which is why we settle for achievable, false peace mondegreens.

False peace is like the Diet Coke version of shalom. It doesn't taste anything like the original and eventually it will kill you, but after a while, you get used to it. Then you get addicted.

Shalom is achieved when every aspect of creation flourishes interdependently, a mutually assured reconstruction. I can have a kind of artificially manufactured diet peace when I lay my sleeping baby down in her crib, knowing she is well, knowing she is safe, knowing she is full, hoping she will sleep through the night. My shallow soul is satisfied by such peace. But shalom will come when I lay my daughter in her crib full, safe, and well—and every other mother can say the same about their own child. Then, and only then, will all be calm and all be bright.

I can have diet peace as long as the walls of my gated community shield me from proximity to the needs of my neighbors; I can have artificial peace as long as soundproof walls are strong enough to silence others' wails; I can have manufactured peace as long as the missiles don't fall on my house, however many other mothers' homes they may destroy. Peace, as it is commonly understood in North American churches and communities, is a copy of a copy of a copy. It's been translated and reproduced beyond recognition. It's a devastating and destructive mondegreen. And shalom is a word we don't even recognize. A protest march lamenting murder and crying out for justice crushes mondegreen peace, and that protest is the first essential step on the path to shalom.

In three of the Gospels, Jesus gives a long teaching on life in his kingdom that Christians call the Sermon on the Mount. In all three versions, it begins with a series of observations that are incomprehensible without an understanding of shalom. In lieu of wrestling and responding to them, we invent a category for them. We declare them "the beatitudes" and label them poetry. But before he can teach anyone how to follow him, Jesus has to tell us where he is going. His introduction is a declaration: He is ushering in God's kingdom, here and now. Forevermore, the weak and meek, the spiritually clueless, the poor, the powerless, the grieving, those hungry for food and thirsty for justice, and the persecuted are blessed. He does not say they *will* be blessed; he says they *are* blessed. But the present tense makes no sense.

Objectively, being poor and powerless and persecuted is the opposite of good fortune. But Jesus's kingdom is shalom, real peace. In the realm where Jesus is king, there is mutually interdependent, universal flourishing. Jesus's kingdom is a welfare state where all fare well. Here in our world, it is good fortune to be powerful and protected and wealthy. But in Jesus's kingdom, goodness is not a scarce quantity bestowed at the top that trickles down the hierarchy. In Jesus's kingdom, goodness grows in crushed hearts, and those identified by the categories of the beatitudes are blessed there.

And where is the kingdom of God? That's what the Pharisees in Luke 17 wanted to know. They came asking Jesus, in essence, "So when is it coming, your crazy 'kingdom'? Where will we find it? What exactly are its boundaries? Where is this place where goodness comes to those who have not earned it and do not deserve it?"

And Jesus said something beatitude-level crazy in response. He said, "The kingdom of God does not come with your careful observation, nor will people say here it is or there it is, because the kingdom of God is within you" (Luke 17:20; my translation). In the clunkiest, most literal translation, he tells them that the kingdom of God is "in the midst of you" or "in the space between you."

Wherever you are, whenever you live, if you are part of Jesus's kingdom, then around you the poor and powerless and persecuted will be blessed. Suffering and injustice will not be fully eradicated by your effort or action, and blessing might not be the only thing suffering ones experience, but citizens of the kingdom of heaven will be a blessing to those crushed by the realms of this earth.

In that same introductory section of the Sermon on the Mount, Jesus says that peacemakers, shalom makers, will be called children of God. And he follows that up with another beatitude: "Blessed are you when people persecute you and curse you and beat you and torture you" (Matt 5:11; my translation). If you are a shalom maker, if you cry out for holy justice and sacred righteousness in the streets, then those empowered by false peace will come for you. They will not call you a peacemaker but a disturber of the peace. They'll say you are a rabble-rouser, troublemaker, and terrorist. They will say that you threaten the very fabric of society. And they will be right about that.

We've largely lost shalom in our church culture and theological imaginations, and that means we have lost our way as salt and light in our communities. Too often, powerful and safe Christians seek to maintain the status quo and protect their advantage instead of following Jesus. Many white Christians label discussions of racial injustice "divisive" and deride and dismiss those who grieve over murder as "woke." But the actual slaughter of Black men, women, and children doesn't disturb our mondegreen peace.

For too many of us, injustice is like Schrodinger's cat: It only exists if we talk about it.

* * *

On the coast of the city of Accra in Ghana, there are two castles that were built to hold enslaved humans until their kidnappers could transport them to colonies in the "New World." In each castle was a portal known as the Door of No Return. Eventually, enslaved people who survived brutal captivity in the dungeons of the castles would be chained and led through those doors. As they crossed the threshold, they would take their last step on African soil. There was no return after they passed through. They would never come back to their land, to their families, or to their culture again.

Haunting, too, is what the enslavers built above the engineered evil of that door. Over the door of no return, they built a sanctuary. People gathered to worship God in a room they named a "sanctuary" and saw no unholy irony in the thick walls, designed in such a way that their peace would not be disrupted by the anguished cries of people they held in captivity below. Those who led worship in such a sanctuary could preach the peace of empire, they could preach Pax Romana, they could preach the peace of Pharaoh, and they could even preach the peace of progress and civilization. But they could not preach shalom. Shalom would destroy that sanctuary, and all the hell it was built to pseudo sanctify. And that destruction would liberate God's children above and beneath.

A chant can't disrupt what does not exist. "No Justice, No Peace" is the truth that will set us free. But many of us fear those who cry out for shalom. We do not think it's possible. We fear it would be worse than what we have. Our fear of conflict and rejection is greater than our desire for God's will to be done on earth as it is in heaven. Our love of comfort and personal safety is greater than our love for our neighbors. No one fares well here.

But the word of God, in Scripture and made flesh, testifies that another way is possible, even here. Jesus calls us to radical new life, which is to say, back to our roots, to the ancient first ways of living together in wholeness and delight. We've lost an essential part of our own story, whole portions of our spiritual alphabet. But the Lord assures us that once we go seeking it—once we line up with all the other riffraff behind the ones who lead us into a future we've never known but always longed for, and once we learn to walk by faith and lean not on our impoverished understanding—we will be found.

3

KINSHIP

We Belong to One Another

WHAT WOULDN'T YOU do for your child? Your mother? Your sibling? Would you give them a kidney? Would you let them move in if they had nowhere else to go? Would you loan them money—or maybe just give it to them? Would you help them find a job? Help them rewrite their resume, reach out on their behalf to a contact, drive them to the interview? When you realize they need a new suit for the interview, would you put it on your credit card? Would you drink a beer together afterward because it went well—or because it didn't?

When you realize you haven't heard from family in a while, do you call to check in? Do you reply to every text immediately? Do you send them jokes and pictures just because you thought of them? Do you carry them around with you in your heart? If they were ill, would you sit by their hospital bed even though the smell of the place makes you nauseous? If the time comes, will you plan the funeral but ask others to speak, because you know you won't be able to?

Your answers were likely yes to most or all these questions. Your loved one is flesh of your flesh, bone of your bone, forever part of your story, and not even death will part you. What wouldn't you do for your family?

Your *immediate* family. But what about a grandparent, an aunt or uncle, a cousin? Would you give them a kidney if they needed it? Maybe, but only after intense consideration. How long could *they* stay in your home? Would you help them to find a job? Yes, but maybe not as urgently. You'd visit the hospital, yes, absolutely. But to chat and give the inner circle a break, you wouldn't need to stay overnight. You'd be honored to speak at the funeral. You'd agonize over the perfect words. Each year, you might pour one out for them on their birthday.

What about a really good neighbor? A longtime friend? A promising new acquaintance? If tragedy shattered their lives, what would you do for them?

Now the calculus of love changes again. No one expects a kidney, but maybe a DoorDash gift card? Would you make sure to roll their trash cans back up from the curb? Would you make it a point to drop off a casserole with a note? Would you tuck in a slim devotional book, if you want to go deep, if they're into that kind of thing? What would you do? You'd find a gesture that would signal that you are a good, caring person. You'd go to the funeral and hug the family in the receiving line. You'd think of them fondly, whenever you happened to think of them.

What would you do for a stranger? Or someone you see as a miserable loser who keeps bringing misfortune on themselves? Or someone you hate? Give a kidney, are you crazy? Open your home? Get financially involved? Spend your social capital on someone you don't know or wish you didn't? None of that. When tragedy strikes them, you shake your head, maybe make jokes about karma. Maybe you ask God to forgive you for not being sorry. You wouldn't go to the funeral if there was one. Because they weren't part of your life, because you are glad that they're gone.

What do you do for family, no matter what, that you wouldn't do for those who aren't?

There's a weird and troubling story in Luke that we pastors all stumble over. Jesus is teaching in somebody's house, and it's crowded. No one else can fit inside. But a message can, and it reaches Jesus at the center of the room: "Your mother and your brothers are outside." And Jesus says, essentially, no they're not. He says, "My mother and my brothers are those who do the will of God." My brothers and mother are right here in this room. Apparently Jesus didn't get the family-first memo.

Another time a woman comes and falls before Jesus in worship and adoration and screams out, "Blessed is the womb that bore You and the breasts which nursed You!" (Luke 11:27–28; NKJV). This is already awkward. There's really no good way for a person to respond to that. But incredibly, Jesus finds a way to make it even more uncomfortable. "No; blessed rather are those who hear the word of God and keep it." Oh. Okay. Ouch.

In the last chapter, we discovered that our vision of peace is narrower and smaller than God's. Could the same be true of our understanding of family?

* * *

In 2014, Harvard University released a study ranking the economic mobility in major US cities. Charlotte, the city where I've lived since 2004, ranked fiftieth out of fifty. This means a child born poor in Charlotte is less likely to escape poverty than a child born poor in any other US city. To put it bluntly, in Charlotte, you only need to know one thing about a person's past to see their future: their zip code. If you know which part of the city a person grew up in, you can predict their economic future with damning accuracy.

Some of Jesus's most troubling teaching concerns wealth. It's unfathomable to us, but Jesus sees money as a spiritual liability, not an asset. Now don't twist this: That doesn't make poverty a spiritual advantage. Life is challenging enough without having to constantly worry about being evicted, losing childcare, finding reliable transportation, affording lifesaving medicines like insulin, or paying basic bills even after working eighty hours a week for minimum wage. Managing wealth and surviving poverty are both soul consuming. It is destructive to have too much or too little. Still, if we had a choice, we all know what we'd choose.

The economic apartheid in Charlotte is particularly damning because we also have one of the highest concentrations of churches per capita in the country. Drive around Charlotte and the only thing you'll see more often than a church is a storage unit. We love our Jesus and we love our stuff, and we won't let go of either, no matter how hard they are to integrate into our daily life. And apparently, we love both Jesus and our stuff more than we love our poor neighbors.

The thing is, if you are born into one of Charlotte's wealthy or middle-class zip codes, you probably don't know any poor people. Americans are unlikely to have personal relationships with anyone whose life does not closely resemble their own. Our zip codes are not just our destinies but our relational boundaries. Children in poor families go to school with other children in poor families. Children in wealthy families go to school with other children in wealthy families. They grow up to befriend and marry one another.

It's not that there is no interaction. There is professional overlap. Children who grow up in poverty often grow up to be employed by children who grew up in wealthy families. Children in wealthy families often grow up to staff philanthropic or government agencies serving impoverished clients. But peer-to-peer, voluntary relationships like friendship, romantic partnerships, or business collaborations are rare. You might be friendly, but you aren't friends. You might love the way "your" house cleaner cleans your house, but you don't love her. Saying she's "just like family" might make you feel good about yourself, but that doesn't make it true.

Generally, the only way a person born in an impoverished zip code becomes relationally connected to a person born in a wealthy zip code is if the economic circumstances of either person changes. A person born wealthy who becomes poor enters into new communities; a person born poor who becomes wealthy gains access to new communities; but people of diverse economic resources rarely form authentic interpersonal relationships across that divide.

Incriminatingly, this is especially true in Christian churches. Schools and sports teams have scholarships for children they deem exceptional. Churches don't. Most American churches are homogenous, affinity-based communities. Like attracts like. Doctors and lawyers worship with doctors and lawyers. Retail workers and home health aides worship with retail workers and home health aides—that is, when they aren't required to work on Sunday mornings.

When the church I serve was teetering on the edge of death, I had an incredibly honest conversation with a woman in our congregation who I still consider a friend. I'll call her Jill. She came to me to explain why she and her family would be leaving the church, even though she affirmed the values we were trying to embody. The Sunday before, a woman named Vickie had joined us for worship. We all knew Vickie because we saw her frequently at stoplights near the church, holding a sign telling her neighbors that she was hungry and needed money for food. We had welcomed her as an overnight guest several times when we participated in a community-wide temporary shelter program serving unhoused folks in the winter months. But that morning Vickie didn't ask anyone for anything. She didn't come seeking food or shelter. She came like the rest of us. She joined us for worship.

A few days after that, Jill asked if she could meet with me. She tearfully explained that she and her family were leaving to begin the search for a new church, because all the change was just too much. I thought she was disturbed by the shift to contemporary music or the move away from formal ceremonial language in the worship services. But it wasn't the music or the liturgy changes themselves. It was those whom the changes attracted to the community. She explained, "I don't mind serving someone like Vickie, but I don't want to go to church with her. I just want to go to church with my friends."

I don't share this story to shame my friend. Her honesty and self-awareness are rare and exceptional gifts. She wasn't proud of her truth, but she wasn't denying it either. She knew if she worshipped with Vickie, she ran the risk of becoming friends with Vickie. And that friendship, even the chance of it, would make her uncomfortable with the privilege and stability of her life. It would make enjoying her blessings—well, less enjoyable. She was leaving to find a new church like the church she'd always known, where all her friends would have what she had. All she knew of Christian friendship she had learned, Sunday by Sunday, in congregations like ours. I believe she had a deep, foundational misunderstanding of the way of Christ, but I know that it is one she was carefully taught. And I know it was taught to her by pastors like me.

American Christian churches teach that we all belong to Christ, but only rarely do they teach that we belong to each other. Jill and Vickie are both white women. My friend was eager to worship with Black and Latino neighbors; she just couldn't imagine how she could be friends with someone who was poor.

Economic segregation is rarely acknowledged. And that matters, because we need one another to become our real selves.

It wasn't always this way.

* * *

The first Christian communities were remarkable not for their doctrine but for their radical love. This love for one another birthed inconceivable diversity in their communities. Jews and Greeks, men and women, rich and poor, enslaved and enslaver: People of every kind of identity began to gather together in their homes, share their resources, and create a new culture and identity together. And those relationships reformed the foundations of their lives.

For much of my life as a pastor in a Southern church, I have preached under a cloud of suspicion that I don't take the Bible literally enough. So I was particularly astonished one day when an angry member of my community cornered me in my office and admonished me for teaching that the description of the early church found in Acts 2:42–45 should be the model of our new life together. The verses read that believers "devoted themselves to the apostles' teaching and to fellowship, to the breaking of bread and to prayer. Everyone was filled with awe at the many wonders and signs performed by the apostles. And the believers were together and had everything in common. They sold property and possessions to give to anyone who had need."

My accuser was nearly purple with rage when he shouted at me, "That's not true; you can't say we have to do that. They couldn't have done that! If they sold everything, then how did they still have houses to meet in, huh?"

We aren't fazed by the idea that in the early church people just like us worked miraculous signs and wonders. But it threatens the hell out of us to think that back in the day people shared their money, their homes, and their stuff.

Yet people did. Because they believed that in Christ, they were family. Not metaphorical but actual family. When Jesus said, "My mother and brothers are right here in this room," he wasn't trying to provoke people or stir up controversy. He was telling the truth. He was saying: My family includes all the people who hear and practice the word of God; it's not limited to the people who share my DNA.

Following Jesus didn't require people to sever ties with their biological families. One of Jesus's first miracles was to heal Peter's mother-in-law, so clearly disciples maintained close contact with their families. Brothers followed Jesus together, and the famous tension between sisters Mary and Martha existed because they served Jesus as a family. People brought their children to be blessed by Jesus, because whole families came into his community. When he was teaching people how to approach God, there was always a child around for Jesus to pull into the circle and say, "Hey, be like this child." Following Jesus didn't end the family system; following Jesus radically expanded it. Suddenly, family was no longer limited to those who shared blood and buildings. In Christ, family became anyone who shares values and practice. In Christ, family could be anyone.

The inexplicable diversity of the early church signaled the radical power of the grace of Jesus. In the very beginning, everyone assumed Jesus would be returning no later than next Tuesday. In the face of cosmic recreation, differences in culture and class seemed imminently transcendable, because people anticipated the end of all the structures and systems around them. They believed life as they understood it was passing away. Pharisees, tax collectors, peasants, Samaritan women, and Roman centurions found belonging through their shared belief that Jesus was the Messiah. In the midst of their diversity, they found an ultimate spiritual unity in their hope that his transcendent kingdom was immediately on the horizon.

The folks who gathered in these first churches were the opposite of doomsday preppers. Their passionate belief in Christ's way compelled them to center their lives on radical generosity, not radical hoarding. They were consumed with the desire to share their rich treasure with their newfound family, no matter what it cost them. They refused to hold anything back, not even their lives. Far from encouraging them to protect themselves from their enemies, the church cast such a beautiful vision of shalom and enemy reconciliation that believers were eager to imitate Christ and make themselves vulnerable to their enemies, even at the risk of death, so they could widen the circle and welcome more prodigal family members home. They had so adopted the lifestyle of the outrageously loving Father that they were filled with compassion and ever ready to run toward and embrace long lost kin even when they were "still a long way off" (Luke 15:20).

The New Testament letter we call 1 Peter was written to a church whose believers were enduring intense persecution. The letter encouraged them not to be frightened. It reassured them that no one would want to harm them for seeking the good of everyone around them.

But it also prepared them. If they were threatened and harmed for doing good, that was a blessing, because it made them just like Christ. The letter included instructions for those who would be arrested and sentenced to death to "always be ready to give an account for the hope that is within you" (1 Pet 3:15; my translation). The radical power of the reconciling love of Christ meant that even those who were about to kill you could, in a moment, become your family members, ready to lay down their lives for you.

* * *

But when Jesus didn't immediately return in the way people anticipated, cracks appeared in the church. As the delay continued, those cracks widened. Christians began to import the divisions of society into the church. The apostle Paul was horrified to learn that wealthy members of his church in Corinth invited their social peers to gather early for worship—which was hosted in their homes, after all—and set the Lord's table with their preferred dishes. These acts constituted a first-century version of priority elite boarding pass for worship. By the time people in economy class were welcomed aboard the worship plane, the first class was drunk, and only crumbs and dregs were left of the Lord's Supper.

Paul railed at the selfishness and insensitivity of the "first-class" worshippers, who believed common life could be found only with those who shared their wealth and elite social class. He was astonished, and not in a good way, at their pride-fueled assumption that they should have priority access to the grace of God. He marveled at their ignorance, at how completely they'd misunderstood the revelation of Christ. They had desecrated the Lord's Supper by making it one more place of division and separation. He went so far as to say that those who distorted the community around the Lord's Supper in this way were guilty of sinning against Jesus himself.

Then and now, we do not have the power to change the shalom of God or limit the radical scope of reconciliation. But as believers, we do have the power to cheat ourselves out of enjoying it. We can manipulate ourselves into desired positions and portions, but at the cost of grace.

The Corinthians believed they'd improved their worship experience by shutting out the poor, but really, they'd simply distanced themselves from the presence of Christ. By hoarding the physical bread, they'd lost the spiritual bread. They would settle for being Christian benefactors, standing back from the table already full when "those people" showed up to eat.

Christ did not come so that we could create a pious version of the stratified culture that already exists. Paul called out privileged believers for creating a "second seating" for those with whom they did not wish to share a meal.

The contemporary American church takes stratification even further and creates entirely separate ministries and agencies to "deal with" those whose presence makes the privileged uncomfortable. But Jesus has only one table. He came to open our eyes to see that those we are desperate to distance ourselves from are our family. Those whose lives do not mirror our own are not problems to be solved but precious companions on a common journey. No one at the table is a spiritual obligation for anyone else. In Christ, all are beloved friends.

* * *

When I was much younger, I served as an associate pastor of an exhausting, anointed congregation in South Boston. It was a church that struggled beautifully to be the body of Christ, transcending lines of ethnicity, class, and culture. It was flawed and faithful, real and imperfect, and it was in that place that I learned to long for the community conformed to the kingdom of God, not the culture of this world. I frequently left worship exhilarated, which felt wonderful. But equally as frequently, I left worship uncomfortable and discontented, which was valuable.

And I've never left worship in more discomfort than the day two young people, twins from the neighborhood, stood up to give their testimony. When the pastor invited Annie and Peter up to share, I was surprised and excited. I didn't know them well, but I had just started serving with the youth. A shameful part of me wondered if they were going to stand up and bear witness to what a difference I'd already made in their lives.

What they did instead was face all of us who had gathered for worship, all of us who'd spent the last hour lifting our voices in common songs of kindness and unity and generosity and radical, self-giving love, and tell us that their mother had been diagnosed with incurable kidney disease. She had exhausted all treatment options. Her only hope was a kidney transplant, and they were too young to donate. They stood up in the front of the sanctuary and asked their church family to be tested to see if one of us might be a match. And if by a miracle we were, would we give her a kidney? They told us they believed that God would save their mother through us.

And not only was I unwilling to be tested; I was offended they'd asked. Really, I was offended that the senior pastor had *allowed* them to ask—that he had put all of us in this uncomfortable position. I felt it was inappropriate. Maybe I'd consider giving a kidney if a member of my own family, or very close friend, needed one. But, well, I was there to serve Peter and Annie, and there were boundaries that needed to be maintained to keep everyone safe. I was willing to be Christian family with them but not "I'll give you my kidney if you need it" family. As far as I know, no one in the church donated a kidney. I don't know what happened to Peter and Annie's mother.

At that point in my life, I'd finished seminary and passed all my ordination exams. I was a certified Presbyterian pastor, and I was there to serve the youth and children in the neighborhood, to mentor them and nurture them in the faith. But now I realize that I barely knew the Lord then. When two fourteen-year-old twins, facing the loss of the only flesh-and-blood family member they had, stood up and asked me to be family to them, I looked away. I knew who my mother and brothers were, and it was not yet those who were in the room. It was not yet all those who hear and do the word of God.

When my friend came to tell me she was leaving the church all those years later, I wasn't mad, and I didn't blame her. I was sad and ashamed. I blamed myself and all the pastors like me who had failed to be honest about the breadth and depth and cataclysmic, reorienting power of Christ. We had taught her to be a good church member in her confirmation class, but we had lied to her about how very much it would cost her to follow Jesus. Since Constantine's conversion, many of us have devoted almost all our energy to building churches and charities, not disciples. We want to attract people, the right kind of people, and we preach and teach and minister accordingly. We lie and preach that Jesus will make your life *better* instead of making your life *new*. We may have inherited the churches we longed for, but we have not yet recovered our identity in the family of Christ. We've used our reformed theology and orthodox doctrine to disconnect ourselves from the radical nature of kinship. We've hunkered down in theological bunkers to protect ourselves from the way Jesus is reforming our families, and we'll stay stagnant and stuck in them until we recognize and treat as beloved kin all of those who are made in the image of God.

Jesus does not require us to forsake our families, but he does radically expand them in ways that unmoor us. These days we're more subtle and severe than the rich Corinthians. We no longer issue separate invitations to undesirables we desire to distance ourselves from. Now we build entirely distinct organizations to serve them—and then give ourselves humanitarian awards. We settle for mission projects when we could have kinship community. We allow our zip codes, instead of the cross, to form our futures and our families.

When we belong to Jesus, we belong to one another. When we drink from the cup of salvation, we become kin with the whole of unholy humanity. This is the uncomfortable, disorienting truth that sets us free. No matter who we shut out, no matter who we disassociate ourselves from, it is ever and always Christ.

4

TRINITY

Healing from Hierarchy

THE BAPTISM OF Jesus is weird and problematic. All the gospel writers include an account of Jesus coming to the Jordan River and participating in a revival movement led by a prophet called John the Baptist, who just happens to be his first cousin. As his name suggests, baptism was the central feature of John's ministry.

John grew into a wildly holy and incredibly strange prophet. He went back to nature and lived off the grid. He wore animal skins and ate bugs and spent his days pacing up and down the Jordan River, screaming that the kingdom of God was coming. He called people to repent of their sins and be baptized for spiritual cleansing.

This is all well and good, except that he stepped on everyone's toes. For generations, the Hebrew people had a way of handling sin and forgiveness: worship and ritual sacrifice in the very Temple where the angel Gabriel announced John's unlikely birth. The baptizing prophet made a name for himself calling people to return to God by leaving the sanctuary. He declared that the Holy One was not in the Temple but in the wilderness. John preached that righteousness couldn't come through the ancient orthodox rituals of animals sacrificed on an altar. He cried out that righteous living could come only through the reign of the long-awaited messiah, who was born to inaugurate the kingdom of heaven on earth.

Strangely enough, many of the religious leaders John's movement attempted to render obsolete came to the desert to hear this firebrand preacher. Even more peculiarly, many of them appeared moved and ready to wade into the water and be baptized with the hoi polloi.

Except, even more oddly, John will have none of it. He will not accept their validation of his ministry. He bars them from participating. In his eyes, they are too sinful to repent. He calls them a brood of vipers and is furious that someone has warned them of the destruction he believes is awaiting them in the kingdom of heaven. Conventional wisdom said that these holy ones John rejected were the elite, preeminent, most righteous, and most faithful members of the nation; but there is nothing conventional about John, and he is too passionate to be wise. He sees a holy inversion of the status quo coming, and he relishes it. John is certain that the messiah will separate the priests and scribes out from the masses—not to lift them up or show them deference in the ways they've come to expect but to sweep them away like garbage into the eternal incinerator.

And as if this rhetoric wasn't terrifying enough, John adds an eschatological coda: "I'm here baptizing you with water for the repentance of sins, but the one who is coming after me—and I'm not even worthy to carry his sandals—he's going to baptize with the Holy Spirit and fire." In other words, "If you think *I'm* infuriated by your sin and hypocrisy, if you think *I'm* scary, just wait 'til you see the One coming after me. He's even more extreme than I am!"

John's ministry was wildly threatening and controversial in his day, but it's not what makes the story of Jesus's baptism problematic for most Christians. The trouble for church people starts when Jesus actually shows up. It turns out he's not there to call out or burn up anybody. He came, saw the line for baptisms, went to the back, and joined in.

And that's what bothers us. Christians believe that Jesus is the Son of God. We believe that Jesus was perfect and without sin. We believe that the righteousness of Jesus is so vast and powerful that through it, God accomplished the salvation and redemption of all creation. So how in the world does it make sense that Jesus, who we believe *is* the Messiah, would choose to be part of a ritual of repentance and renewal and preparation *for* the messiah?

If John was born to announce the coming of the messiah, and Jesus is the Messiah who has come, how does this make any sense? If John's mission was to prepare people to enter into the kingdom over which Jesus reigns, then why would Jesus come out to the middle of the desert where John is holding revivals and ask to be baptized? Does Jesus not know that he's Jesus?

If Jesus is who we think he is, then he should stride onto the scene and push John aside and assume center stage. He should display his greater righteousness in contrast to John's lesser righteousness. John is the warm-up act; Jesus is the headliner. Why isn't Jesus scornfully putting John in his place in the same way John theologically checked the Sadducees and Pharisees? Why would a person who knew he was Almighty God allow himself to be ministered to imperfectly?

It makes no sense to us, or to John. In one of the Gospels, John actually tries to stop Jesus from being baptized. He protests, "I need to be baptized by you, and do you come to me?" (Matt 3:14).

It's a head-scratching moment for regular people, but it drives theologians and biblical scholars crazy. Commentators, ancient and modern, tie themselves into knots trying to explain how even though Jesus "submits" to baptism by John, he didn't need it. They acknowledge that the baptism happened but then list a million reasons why it doesn't mean anything. They tell us it is imperative that we know that even though John says his baptism was for forgiveness of sins, and even though Jesus asks to be baptized, that wasn't an admission of guilt. Jesus didn't have any sins; he was righteous and holy. He got baptized, but he didn't *need* to. So don't get it twisted, okay?

Most importantly, the experts need us to understand that Jesus is superior to John. Yes, John baptized Jesus, they explain, and of course we all know that the person who baptizes is superior to the person who is baptized, but John is still inferior to Jesus. They point to John's own unwillingness to baptize Jesus for support—"See, even John knew this wasn't right." So yes, it happened. The gospel writers can't be denied. But don't let it change how you see Jesus or John. Scholars talk about this moment like it was the scriptural equivalent to an embarrassing one-night stand. It happened, but it didn't *mean* anything.

Except that it *does* mean something, this moment. Jesus reassures John not only that "it is proper for us to do this" but also that this act will "fulfill all righteousness" (Matt 3:15). Far from meaning nothing, Jesus seems to be suggesting that his baptism means everything. Still, experts tell us: None of this righteousness talk matters as long as we are clear about the hierarchy of it all. John was born to prepare the way for Jesus. Therefore, Jesus is more righteous, more holy, and absolutely perfectly superior to John. And John, even though he's the "dunker" and not the "dunkee," is inferior to Jesus.

But what if Jesus actually meant what he said? What if this moment that challenges our settled understanding of righteousness actually *is* the revelation of true righteousness? What if we consider adding righteousness itself to the long list of things we *thought* we understood until we met Jesus?

Most of us are less interested in understanding the story and more interested in explaining it away. But this moment, unwelcome as it is to us, reveals the culture of Jesus's kingdom. Jesus essentially says, "It is right that I be baptized by you now, because this unexpected and unsettling act fulfills all righteousness." In other words, this baptism is the kind of righteousness Jesus restores to the world. It is a righteousness that disturbs and destroys our orienting principle of hierarchy. Like John, even as we long for an entirely new realm of being, we cannot let go of our foundational belief that some people are just worthless garbage, incompatible with redemption. We believe that some people are intrinsically excluded and the rest of us should line up in order of worthiness, from greatest to least.

Come, Lord Jesus, and build your kingdom here, we pray. But even when and where you do, people will still need to be sorted into ontological categories of better or worse, superior or inferior, worthy or unworthy, redeemable or irredeemable. The current manner of sorting and stacking is insufferable, but you will come and set it straight, and order and decency will finally prevail. On that day, you will make it clear who is above who and who is below who, so that we can begin anew currying favor and exerting power accordingly. We do not object to hierarchy; we object to our place in it.

I'm not interested in explaining this story, because it's not a puzzle; it's a revelation. This moment isn't asking to be solved but to be seen. Jesus's baptism radically reorients our understanding of everything. It reveals new truths about God, ourselves, goodness, and most of all, how righteousness is expressed in a healthy and holy community.

Jesus enters the story, and from the beginning he is showing us what he showed John: I am what you think I am, but I am not who you expected. Jesus requires John to baptize him, reassuring John that now that he, the Messiah, is here, and this baptism is the fulfillment of righteousness.

In a breathtaking moment of foreshadowing for those with eyes to see, Jesus takes a last deep breath and lets himself fall back into waiting arms, surrenders as John pulls him down under the water, and waits until John lifts him back up into the air and he can breathe again. And God confirms Jesus's righteousness, literally and immediately, by tearing open the heavens, sending down the Holy Spirit in the appearance of a dove, and saying so that everyone can hear, "This is my Son, the beloved, in whom I am well pleased" (Matt 3:17; my translation).

We may be unsure and uncomfortable about all of this, but God, clearly and manifestly, is not. In the moment the baptism is completed and righteousness is fulfilled, as John lifts Jesus up, river water streaming from his skin, heaven is poured out, and the Trinity materializes. The Holy Spirit comes down like a dove, and we hear the voice of God the Father claiming a well-loved child. Father, Son, and Spirit are all linked together in this one extraordinary moment of righteousness, surrender, and glory: the Trinity.

Scholars and clergy often tell us that trinity is an ineffable, mystical quality of God's character and God's character alone. But what if that's not so? What if trinity is a way of life that belongs not just to God but to all who return to God?

What if Jesus's baptism is a revelation of the way that the unity of God—Creator, Christ, and Holy Spirit—makes room for each one of us? God does this not by measuring our unworthiness and determining how much intimacy with God we deserve but by coming low to embrace us and all that is lovely and loathsome in us. Here at the banks of the Jordan River is theophany: a visible manifestation of divine righteousness that offends us. Here is the holy, a sacred vulnerability and interdependence that is at first inconceivable to us, then appears obscene to us, and finally terrifies us.

If this moment is the fulfillment of righteousness, if this is a manifestation of the way of Christ, then what if one day we begin to live this way as well? What then?

And the thought of that terrifies us, because we can't imagine any other way. We believe the lie that community requires hierarchy. The strong must have agency, the weak must submit, the righteous must seek out and destroy the unworthy. If we keep trying, we think, someday we'll get our hierarchies absolutely right, and they will heal us. We cling to the life we understand, the ways that leave familiar wounds. We cling, even though Christ at his baptism, at his table, on his cross showed us another way: a way of vulnerability and interdependency that has been lost but could be recovered. We cling to what we know and call it sacred. The status quo, while it can't separate us from God, distorts and severs the sacred bonds between us.

* * *

Get three pastors in a room, and you don't need to supply alcohol; we'll immediately start trading stories. A good friend tells the story of a church member who stood up in a congregational meeting and threatened to go to her car and get her gun and shoot him if a proposed change to worship wasn't voted down. Another friend shares the story of a time a member of her church *licked her face* in the receiving line after worship. Another tells of an angry member repeatedly calling her home at 11 p.m. during the ninth month of her pregnancy, outraged that the hedges surrounding the property had been improperly trimmed. We laugh as we tell these stories, a wholehearted competition for who's had the most difficult assignment.

Almost every church member has their own stories to tell, too—stories about pastors abusing their authority. Let's be clear: Those are the truly heartbreaking ones: The mother who was informed that her son's baptism had been canceled because the new pastor believed baptizing children of unwed parents condoned sin. The pregnant teenager banned from the property of her Christian school because the authorities deemed her apology for promiscuity insincere and determined that her presence on campus was corrupting the innocence and purity of other young people. (Her boyfriend, meanwhile, remained enrolled as a student.) And I'll never forget standing next to a teenage boy in a hallway outside the auditorium of a youth conference; he couldn't meet my eyes, and I struggled to hear his voice as he whispered, "Does that mean I'm a mistake?" because the platformed speaker had repeatedly and definitely declared that sex outside of marriage was never part of God's plan. Sometimes, our warped zeal for righteousness leads us to destroy one another. Sometimes, in our passion to serve Jesus, we wound one another, the very body of Christ.

I have a story I used to love to tell. Very early in my ministry, a church member screamed at me in front of a group of high schoolers because I'd purchased the wrong shade of cream paint. As a brand-new associate pastor, I'd been left in charge while the head of staff went on vacation. Along with regular weekly jobs, I was tasked with hosting a visiting youth group on a mission trip. I was responsible for welcoming them and getting them oriented and gathering all the supplies they needed to finish their projects around the church. Their biggest job that week was giving the fellowship hall a sorely needed fresh coat of paint. My boss told me that I needed to reach out to a man named Louie to get his help selecting the paint.

I don't know how old Louie was but probably not as old as he seemed to me then. A white, gay man with HIV and in recovery from addiction, Louie lived in one of the public housing developments that surrounded the church. I never saw him in anything other than jeans and a pristine T-shirt. In the winter he added a Patriots sweatshirt. He was greyhound thin, face and hands permanently tanned. He wore his hair long, slicked back in a stringy gray ponytail.

He'd found refuge in the congregation, found not just belonging but purpose. He cooked all the meals for our large summer children's ministry programs in the woefully insufficient nonindustrial kitchen, and he whistled while he did it. He handled minor repairs and facility upkeep, almost single-handedly managing to hold the building together with skill, spit, and duct tape. And he planted and tended the garden, a carefully curated oasis of brilliant color behind a chain-link fence, our own Eden in a decaying gray asphalt wilderness. Louie was more than welcome in the church; he was needed.

The last time the hall had been painted he'd done it himself, meticulously prepping the space. He'd carefully selected the precise shade of cream, bright enough to lighten the room but not so white that every ding and smudge would show. Consulting Louie about the logistics was practical: He'd know how much paint to buy, how many brushes we'd need, how best to secure the drop clothes. But it was also *right*, an acknowledgment of all the sacred ways he served and shaped the community.

Not many people had cell phones then, so connecting with Louie wasn't easy. He was meticulous about keeping his promises, but otherwise, he showed up when he showed up. I tried to find out what paint he wanted me to buy. When I couldn't get him on the phone, I walked over to his apartment. But when I couldn't get into the building, I left and bought the paint myself. We weren't looking to change the color, I reasoned, just apply a fresh coat. The hall was cream, so that's what I bought.

And that's what the teens and their advisors were putting on the walls when I got an awkward call from the visiting youth group leader saying that I needed to get to the church right away. I'd bought the wrong color cream, and there was a guy who was really mad about it, and no one knew what to do.

When I arrived, work had stopped. Louie was waiting for me. I stood in the center of a hastily prepped, half-painted room rimmed by privileged teenagers and let him yell at me.

"You know what's wrong with you?" he said. "You think you know *everything* just because you went to seminary. You were told to get my approval on the paint color, but you didn't bother. People like you never think someone like me knows anything that matters!"

I opened my mouth to defend myself, to tell Louie that I'd called, to protest that he didn't have an answering machine so I couldn't leave a message, and to inform him that I'd walked to his building but couldn't get in. Louie stepped closer and got even louder. "This is *not* the right color for these walls! I know what paint color belongs on these walls! The color is Glidden semigloss number 911, and I will always remember because I will never forget that day!"

That was the crescendo moment, but as he stormed out of the building, he turned for one final parting shot. "Who left *you* in charge? We need a *man* in charge of this place!"

Once he was gone, everyone in the room looked at me. I apologized for the scene, told them to keep painting, and got out of there as quickly as possible so no one would see me cry. I was raw. I was devastated. Not only because I'd been embarrassed so publicly, but also because I really liked Louie. On the plus side, the pastor supervising the youth later told me that my abject humiliation had led to a fruitful time of reflection at the group's evening devotions.

Several weeks later in worship, as we were singing the song "Will You Let Me Be Your Servant," Louie came up and put his arm around my shoulders. I knew that was his apology, and I accepted it. We never spoke about what happened. Two years later, I left the church. Just a few years after that, Louie died. Now they can paint the hall any shade of cream they want.

Almost all the adults from the church I knew then have died—of complications from diabetes, from obesity, from AIDS, from high blood pressure, from addiction—but really, they all died from poverty. For a season, though, we were church together.

Louie and I never talked about what happened to one another. That was righteousness in my eyes then. I didn't shout back at him, I didn't defend myself, I swept it under the rug. But I didn't bury the story. I didn't talk about it to Louie, but I sure did talk about it. Not to church members, but to my friends outside the congregation, my peers in seminary, and later, to ministry colleagues. It was my favorite "I can top that" ministry horror story to trade: "Oh yeah? You think that was bad, let me tell you about the time I was chewed out for painting the fellowship hall the wrong shade of cream!"

For years as I told the story, I cast myself as the innocent, passive victim and Louie as the unreasonable aggressor. But the truth is much more complicated. Yes, Louie screamed at me in front of a room full of people. But not because I chose the wrong shade of cream, not because a life of suffering had warped him and not because he was a jerk. He screamed at me because I cut him out.

Louie played an essential role in our community. He was honored for his aesthetic, his expertise, his craftsmanship, and his institutional knowledge. Outside the church he might have been looked at with suspicion as a "poor gay man," but inside our church he was a cherished and important leader. Yet that's not how I made him feel that day. I did what seemed like more than enough to me, but my actions did not communicate honor or belovedness to Louie.

I just went to the store and bought the paint without him, because it didn't really matter to me what color paint went on the walls. In fact, I was proud to be a person who didn't really care what color paint goes on the walls. But what I couldn't see then was that not caring about the paint, not valuing Louie's view and experience, was the same as not valuing *him*. I said I loved and honored Louie because that's what a pastor would say. But words are cheap, and our choices reveal the truths we hide even from ourselves. My choice not to include Louie revealed something about my understanding of ministry, and my choice not to have a painful and difficult conversation about what happened, if I'd had eyes to see it, showed how I understood the body of Christ. Picking paint by myself showed Louie that I didn't really value him as a leader in our community. And that's a pastor's essential job: not to get a room repainted but to care authentically about the people in the room and notice who's missing. What I see now is that I was proud to be in a church with people like Louie because it made me feel righteous. But I wasn't interested in knowing and loving Louie. Really, I was using him.

I think about Louie and that day often. When I look at that story now, what it reveals to me is not that I was a good pastor or Louie was a bad member, but that all of us had an unhealthy hierarchical understanding of church that was alienating us from God and one another.

I didn't make much of an effort to get Louie's help because I was offended and efficient. I was offended because I thought that I was competent to pick out paint all by myself. I resented needing anyone else's approval. I was the associate pastor, which meant that I answered to the head of staff who was "above" me in the organizational chart. Why did I need permission from a church member who was "below" me? I could have tracked Louie down to get his buy-in, but it would have turned an errand into an ordeal. I'd have had to find him and arrange a time and drive him to the store, making myself vulnerable to his schedule. Like all of us, Louie had many talents and many burdens. If I spent time with him, I'd have to *be his pastor*, and all I wanted to do was get to the next task on my list. Which is why I wanted to pick out the damn paint by myself. Which is why he was so hurt and angry. Which is why I owed him an apology as much as he owed me one.

At the very least, we owed one another a chance to tell the truth. Not as a pastor listening to a church member or a church member to a pastor, but as two broken and beloved people bravely communicating how it felt to be rejected and their need for honor, love, and belonging.

All this I know now. Louie apologized to me, in action if not in words, and we both understood that. But what I see now is that we were in a system where my pain was centered and valued by everyone but his wasn't. Something made him that angry, and I was so busy being hurt and offended, so content to cast him as a cartoon villain, that I never bothered to wonder why.

Louie spent his days growing flowers in concrete, preparing food for hundreds of children in a tiny kitchen, and serving a church that, at the time, didn't affirm his full humanity. Why was a man as gentle and generous and kind as that behaving so uncharacteristically? I never wondered about the source of his pain. In my world at that time, Louie existed to make me feel like a good pastor, to make me appear like a caring person. But I wasn't willing to put the work in to actually care about him.

We make time for the people who matter to us. We listen to them. We tell them the truth. We value their gifts. We make space for their contributions, even when it would be easier and more efficient to move on without them. In other words, we meet them where they are, like Jesus met John.

I believe all the things the prophet Isaiah foretold about Jesus: King of kings, Lord of lords, Prince of Peace, Wonderful Counselor, Mighty God, the government will rest upon his shoulders (9:6). I believe all these things, and so I'm trying to see that moment that begins Jesus's public ministry as a herald of the realm of God. I'm trying to truly see that moment, which was the first step on the road to Calvary and the empty tomb, the first push that set the whole Rube Goldberg machine of salvation into perpetual motion. I'm trying to let that moment—when Jesus left Galilee and sought John out on the edge of the Jordan River—show me what righteousness is.

* * *

Jesus came to the Jordan to be baptized by John, who spent his whole life preparing for the righteous messiah. John had a zeal for righteousness that was terrifying. He called the most powerful religious leaders of his day poisonous snakes and told people that God could claim them on the edge of a river just as much as at the edge of an altar. John was infuriated by the injustice and hypocrisy and brutality of the world and longed for the day when the poor would get justice and the oppressors would get what was coming to them.

John, with leather on his back and bugs in his teeth, would rather have been crushed by the system than find a way to survive in it. John saw righteousness in three bright, clean, clear steps. Step one was to call the people to forsake ritual sacrifices and seek real repentance. Step two was to tell priests and teachers to burn in hell. And step three was to be baptized by Jesus, not the other way around.

John understood so much and so little about the kingdom of God.

Jesus came and stood before John in his own scandalously sacred flesh and waited to be baptized. Jesus sought out John to lay him down in the water and lift him up again, foreshadowing all that was to come. Jesus heard John's objections and replied: We will do this now, even though it confuses and offends you, because what it actually does is fulfill all righteousness.

Jesus began his revelatory life not by casting John down or cutting him out but by standing in line. Jesus inaugurated his reign in the moment when he offered up his own flesh to sanctify John's life's work. Jesus saw the sacred beauty of John's faith. He wasn't offended or ashamed of John's limits. Jesus's love isn't limited to perfection. John was a voice crying out in the wilderness that the righteousness of God was coming. He believed that when the long-expected righteousness arrived, it would separate and sear. And Jesus was that righteousness, anticipated but unrecognizable. Born to redeem all that ever was and ever will be, on his way to save the world, and still with all the time in it to meet John where he was and bear witness in love to all that will be.

The kingdom is found wherever righteousness is no longer twisted into a weapon that separates and consumes. The kingdom is wherever righteousness submits and sanctifies. Jesus doesn't skip John. Jesus doesn't discard his cousin as dead weight now that his usefulness has passed. Jesus doesn't show up and say, "That's cute, but who needs your stupid, ignorant baby baptism now that I'm here. I can do it better and faster without you now." Because if "it" is salvation, it involves including John and creating the confusion that makes us question what faithfulness and righteousness will look like from now on.

When you see that Jesus submitting to John's baptism is the fulfillment of all righteousness, that moment becomes a catalyst for new creation in your own life. That moment will make you wonder if righteousness could possibly be more than a competition or scarce commodity or a brutal power that discards and destroys whatever is blemished and scarred. The way Jesus was baptized opens our eyes to see that righteousness isn't a spiritual asset we hoard in our quest to be the greatest one but a pathway to healthy and holy unity. The righteousness displayed in Jesus's baptism is the restored, holy wholeness of interdependency.

In other words, it is trinity.

We see this unity in the moment a Son is lifted up in his cousin's arms, the sky parting, and God's own Spirit descending like a dove. We hear this unity in the voice of God declaring, "You are mine; in you I am well pleased." We feel this unity anytime we stumble into a place where we know we are loved and no longer alone and also that we've found a place where belonging is not at stake and so it is safe here to learn and unlearn, to change and grow. John and the crowd do not see or understand this fulfillment of righteousness. The ones who are served and saved by Jesus do not understand the beauty and power and goodness of his loving submission to the one he loves. But God does. The voice of the Creator says, "This righteousness, which confuses and offends the sin-sick world, deeply pleases me."

As a young pastor earnestly determined to redeem myself by doing ministry impressively and efficiently for Jesus, I passed Louie by. But Jesus detoured and laid himself down in John's arms. And John did not understand. John was so disturbed by his cousin's alternative righteousness that a time came when he wondered if another, better savior was coming. And Jesus and his righteousness are not Tinker Bell: They do not need to be believed in to exist. Even unheralded, Jesus's righteousness is undiminished.

These days, when I hear the word *trinity*, I think of Jesus seeking John out for baptism and the beauty of that righteousness unperceived by human eyes. I think of the Spirit and the Creator breaking open the heavens to rejoice and enter into the glory of the moment. These days when I think of trinity, I remember that day Louie put his arm around me in the sanctuary, and I wish I'd been wiser and braver. I wish I'd followed him out of the room and let him see me cry. I wish I'd been strong enough to show those teenagers just how much it mattered to me that he was angry. I wish I hadn't believed that being a pastor meant pretending that I was too tough to be hurt. I wish I'd loved him enough to make myself vulnerable. I wish after he hugged me, I'd invited him out for coffee and asked him to tell me his side of the story of that day and to listen as I told him mine.

Now I read the story of Jesus coming to John to be baptized and see that no matter who we are, we belong to one another, and righteousness means leaving no one out or behind. I watch Jesus come to John, and I see now that the way we do things matters more than the things we do.

In the moment John raises Jesus up from the water, we see the presence of the triune God: Father, Son, and Holy Spirit. For me, it is not a theological puzzle to be solved but a holy affirmation. In God's realm, the things we could accomplish alone, we do together. The life we could have alone, we create together. This new righteousness we embody especially confuses the rigidly faithful. John wanted to flip the hierarchy; Jesus came to cast out the hierarchy altogether. John wanted to cast out the worthless and to center the worthy; Jesus came to lift up the worthiness of all creation and savor the embrace of all the beloved ones.

The lost revelation of trinity is not an abstract theological doctrine after all but a way of being and becoming in community.

It's the glory of God manifested in loving imperfect people, like Jesus loved John. It's the freedom and flourishing that comes when we have generous and healthy expectations of one another. It is the revelation that conflict too can be a blessing from God that grows good gifts.

Trinitarian community gives us a way to embrace the limits of who we are and what we understand and then to cross that threshold into deeper love and understanding. A church that recovers trinity as an embodied way of being community sinks more deeply into grace-filled dependence on Jesus and one another. In a church that "does" trinity, people see each other as worthy not despite their flaws and needs or because of their gifts and talents but simply worthy in their sheer existence. A church that lives out trinity won't fear conflict or sweep it under the rug, but take time to recover common ground they already know exists for them in Christ. A church that embodies trinity will seek out the presence of God not only in their shiny successes and comforting traditions but also in crisis and confusion, trusting that wherever we've wandered or stumbled, Jesus is there.

Jesus has no greater agenda than to be with people as they are. He is not offended by our incapacity to recognize his righteousness; he opens our eyes to the true nature of holiness. And once we allow him to move us past fearing, using, and being offended by one another, we may discover our deepest union with Jesus is found in the space that separates us from each other.

Part II

HIDDEN

Seeking a God Who Hides

5

THERE IS MORE THAN WE KNOW

THE ELECTRONIC SIGN outside the church around the corner from my home pulses one steady message. I pass it often, and it troubles me every time.

Life is BETTER with Jesus
Jesus makes us BETTER at life!!

No exceptions, no explanations, no exclusions. Just a promise with two exclamation points—"Jesus makes us better at life!!"—that somehow reads like a threat.

The words on the sign bother me, and the words that aren't on the sign bother me even more. I want to ask the sign makers what they mean by *better*. Better for whom? Better than who? Better compared to what? I wonder what it feels like to be battling cancer or grief or living in fear and drive past that sign every day. If your life today isn't better than it was yesterday—if your marriage is falling apart, or you've been fired, or you've discovered your teenager is cutting themselves—does that mean that somehow you've lost Jesus? That he's excused himself to give you a chance to get it together in private?

Can we truly tell how much or how little Jesus we have by measuring how much better our lives are than other people's? Should the people navigating the collapse of their country in Haiti or Ukraine or Syria understand the increasing peril and difficulty of their lives as an indicator that Jesus is with us and not them?

By every standard except moral decency, it was better to be white than Black in the antebellum South. White people had more safety, more agency, and more access to resources than Black or Native Americans. So were the people with the better lives more "with" Jesus than those enduring suffering, injustice, and domestic terrorism?

Or is the sign saying any life is better with Jesus than it would be without? So it's just "better" to be Indigenous and mourn the genocide of your ancestors "with Jesus" than without, "better" to be a Black mother fearing for the safety of her son "with Jesus" than without, "better" to be a white person of privilege "with Jesus" than without? Is any and every configuration of human life rendered "better" by proximity to Jesus, thus relieving everyone of the onus, agency, or urgency to labor for righteousness and justice?

But here's the thing: If pressed, I'd have to admit that I don't entirely disagree with the sign. I'm a pastor, for Christ's sake, so *of course* I believe that a relationship with Jesus positively impacts life. But simplifying the gospel to fit on an electronic sign designed to display the cost of a two-liter bottle of soda is theological malpractice. The trouble with the "Jesus makes us BETTER at life" sign is that it's a formula: life with Jesus > life without Jesus.

A good formula can be a gift. In math, formulas are simple, reliable, symbolic articulations of complex phenomena. Mathematical formulas are both revelation and shortcut. They allow us to build on the wisdom of those who have come before, and they allow us to solve problems even without direct experiential knowledge. The Pythagorean theorem is $a^2 + b^2 = c^2$. Every time you plug in the values correctly, the formula will produce the correct answer. You don't have to understand. You only have to correctly apply. Recipes, design theory, Hallmark movies, couch-to-5K plans—these are all formulas that can reliably deliver good taste, pleasing aesthetics, soothing entertainment, and injury-free achievement of a bucket list goal.

My point is that formulas are gifts, except for when they are not. Formulas become toxic when we impose them on the parts of reality that aren't formulaic. When, in pursuit of efficiency and uniformity, we turn our historic, destructive racial biases into criminal justice sentencing guidelines, those formulas become tools of oppression and white supremacy, reliably reproducing racial inequities. When we exploit human vulnerabilities to market opportunities and sell books and conferences promising to share foolproof formulas for happy lives, healthy bodies, loving families, and successful businesses to desperate people, these fake formulas exploit and impoverish the most vulnerable.

When formulas lie, they become a curse. When formulas tell us something difficult and multifaceted is actually simple, straightforward, and universal, they become oppressive chains.

"Life with Jesus is better because Jesus makes us better at life" is formulaic, reductive theology. It further burdens already heavily burdened people. I happen to believe that statement is true *and* that it's dangerously, viciously, ruinously incomplete. Those who put the formula on wayside pulpits may do so intending to lure passersby toward Jesus, but really they've set a trap that plunges seekers into a howling void of abandonment. When we obediently plug our life into the slots and don't get the "better" we were promised, we look around for someone to blame. After all, formulas can't lie. So we grow to hate God or ourselves or our neighbors.

Still, we humans love to live by formulas, not faith. We love to pretend that God is a problem we can solve, an energy we can harness and control, an advantage we can acquire and leverage. We love to approach the holy with a formula that promises us preferred outcomes and predictability.

The Bible has a word for this: idolatry. An idol, often represented in religious rituals by an object, is any ideology created by humans but worshiped as God. We crave control so desperately that we are more than willing to pretend that we have it.

If life is better with Jesus, then whatever makes your life better in your eyes can become your god. Achievement, security, power, pleasure, sexual orthodoxy—whatever makes your life better becomes your savior. And it works until it doesn't. It works until you need it most.

I imagine that almost everyone reading these words will have experienced the pain of discovering the false promises of a god formula. After such disillusionment, it's easy to sneer at those who still believe in holy formulas. It's easy to think we are so much braver and smarter and better for rejecting them. But the reason idolatrous formulas remain so popular is because, as numerous as their faults are, the alternative—vulnerably worshiping God—often appears so much worse to us. Odds are, much as we scornfully reject a formulaic god, we hate the alternative even more.

What could be worse than a formula god we know isn't real or true? A real God who is a mystery. A real God who often is hidden.

* * *

Ironically, Scripture—the revelation of God—is very clear about the hiddenness of God. The Bible, which people of faith believe is the word of God given to reveal God to humanity, declares the absence of God as much as God's presence.

Psalm 13 begins with the anguished cry, "How long, Lord? Will you forget me forever? How long will you hide your face from me?" Similarly, Psalm 22 erupts in a howl of despair that Jesus knew and screamed from the cross, "My God, my God, why have you forsaken me?" The prophet Jeremiah, speaking for God, declares that no one should bother praying anymore because "I will not listen when they call to me in the time of their distress." Lamentations 3:44 describes God wrapping God's self in a cloud that no prayers can penetrate. The prophet Isaiah declares, "Truly you are a God who has been hiding himself, the God and Savior of Israel" (45:15). Ezekiel is caught up in a prophetic trance to witness the spirit of the Lord leave the Temple in Jerusalem explaining that "because you have defiled my sanctuary with all your detestable things and with all your abominations, therefore I will withdraw" (Ezek 5:11; my translation).

In Mark, every time Jesus is correctly identified as the Messiah, he responds by commanding the speaker, whether human or spirit, not to tell anyone. Biblical scholars have labeled this phenomenon the "messianic secret." Jesus may be the light of the world, but in Mark he demands to remain hidden.

Job famously describes a faithful and devoted believer's thwarted attempt to know and understand God in the midst of unanticipated suffering. While the book rejects the formulaic consolation speeches of his friends as blasphemy and declares Job's complaints and his questions sacred speech, it also portrays God's freedom to remain a mystery. Maddeningly, God refuses to answer Job's theological questions, even as he commends Job for asking them. Despite what you might surmise from the ubiquitous saying "the patience of Job," in chapter after chapter Job shakes his fist and screams, "You owe me an explanation, God!" In the end, God shows up in a whirlwind and says, essentially, "Consider the majesty of the hippopotamus" and "No, I don't." It's not a satisfying answer to the problem of suffering, but it's the only real answer we have.

The biblical mandate, over and over again, is to seek the Lord. Seek the Lord and live. But what are you doing when you seek? You are looking for what is hidden. First Samuel 3 opens with the sober assessment that, in those days, the word of the Lord was *yiqqar*: rare and hidden. It doesn't say the people stopped listening and perceiving; Scripture says God mostly stopped speaking. When God calls out to young Samuel in the temple, the boy cannot recognize God's voice. Why? Because God had not been speaking. God had been hiding.

A God who hides from those who seek God is inscrutable enough. But Scripture is also full of stories of people finding God in ridiculous places, and in times they weren't even looking. Moses encounters the presence of God in a burning bush, an ordinary desert plant inflamed by the presence of God, on fire but not consumed. Moses isn't seeking God, but there God is, waiting to be stumbled upon. Famously, when Moses turns aside to investigate this theophanic manifestation, clearly strategically designed to entice Moses, God coaxes him closer. The flames begin to whisper his own name, "Moses, Moses." But as soon as God in the bush beckons him closer, God warns him to stay back: "Come no closer." So which is it? Should he come closer or stay back? Both.

Later, much later, Exodus recounts God's custom of descending to meet with Moses in the tent of meeting, to talk with the prophet "face to face, as one speaks to a friend" (Exod 33:11). And yet just a few verses after describing the ritual, God warns Moses that no one can see his face and live. When Moses, seeking reassurance, asks to see the glory of God, God places Moses in the cleft of a rock and covers Moses's face with a holy hand, explaining that "I will put you in a cleft in the rock and cover you with my hand until I have passed by. Then I will remove my hand and you will see my back; but my face must not be seen" (Exod 33:22–23).

The burning bush calls Moses closer, then warns he's come too close. Moses is God's friend, talking with God face to face—but no one can see God's face and live.

How can all these things be true? Biblical criticism bluntly answers that it can't, that such contradictions are the exposed seams of merged sacred texts. Maybe so, but the contradictions are also profoundly true. We can both know God intimately and not know God at all. The spirit of God manifests in our life and calls out our name, drawing us closer only to warn us to back off. God can be known; God is near. God is a mystery; God is hidden. Both cannot be true. And still, they are. Modern theology seeks to explain all this in a way that makes it, if not appealing, at least reasonable. Testimony simply bears witness that it is so.

Before the dominions of this world co-opted Christ as mascot and revenue source, theologians spoke honestly, if mysteriously, about the hiddenness of God. Church fathers and mothers wrote about *Deus absconditus*: the fundamental unknowability of the essence of God. This is not the God we would choose. This is not the God we would create. But the witness of Scripture is clear: This is the God we have. God is incarnate. God is with us. God is near. And also, God is hidden. God must be sought. God often seems absent. We insist it must be one way or the other, but the saints and Scripture testify otherwise. God is an intimate mystery.

You cannot market this. You cannot sell access to an unknowable God. We have glimpses, we have authentic, astonishing revelations, and we can grow more and more like God. And yet, ever and always, we will have more to discover. We can protest, we can pretend, but we cannot reduce God to human comprehensibility. Acknowledging that God is a mystery isn't an admission that we know nothing. It is a wise and humble admission that we cannot know everything. The hiddenness of God is why we are enjoined to walk by faith and not by sight. Were we able to know the fullness of God on this side of eternity, we'd have no need of faith. Faith, hope, and love abide, Paul concludes in his Corinthian love poem, but the greatest of these is love (1 Cor 13:13). Why? Because of these three, love alone is eternal. When we finally see face-to-face, we will no longer need faith, and we will have nothing left to hope for. Until then, we love the God we cannot fully know.

God is ever and always a burning bush, light and warmth and presence that cannot be denied and cannot be explained. A fire that doesn't consume us, a fire that transforms us, a holy fire that we do not initiate or control.

But there is something quintessentially human that rejects a hidden God and the vulnerability that loving such a God requires. We insist that God can be fully known, maybe not by everyone but certainly by us. We demystify the mystery and worship only what seems reasonable and sacred in our eyes. We will not trust the Lord but will lean on our own understanding—which we cleverly concentrate into formulaic slogans. We declare "I don't know" the three most blasphemous words, and we only follow leaders who never say them. To every question, there must be an answer we can understand, even if it's ugly, even if it's dangerous. To every problem, there is a solution we can execute. To every season, there is a task to be accomplished and an enemy to be blamed. This is the way we bind ourselves to the false gods we've constructed.

The only way to free our lives of idols and formulas is to accept, even reluctantly, that we are called to follow a God who hides. This is a deep and holy irony.

* * *

As a Christian, I celebrate the incarnation. I am compelled and consoled by the startling truth that Almighty God chose to be born among us because God desires intimacy with us. I believe God chose to walk around on earth wrapped in human flesh in order to close the distance between created and Creator. And yet Jesus the Christ used his human mouth to implore us to seek the kingdom of God, and to seek the kingdom first. God is here. God is not here.

Jesus told us to seek the kingdom even though, again and again, he declared that the kingdom had come, even that it was in the midst of us. The kingdom is here, and yet we must seek it. God is near, and God is hidden. This isn't the God I want. This isn't the God I understand. But this *is* the God I recognize. The more I grow in knowing God, the more my awareness of all of God I do not know grows. The answer to this is not despair.

Well, maybe sometimes it is—but not only or always.

Jesus of Nazareth invites us into the mystery of God, beckons us closer, encourages us. Ask, seek, knock. Those who ask will be answered, those who seek will find, the door will be opened to those who knock. But those whose souls are satisfied with idols, slogans, and formulas have no questions to ask, no intimacy to seek, no doors they long to open. And so they remain on the outside, where there is wailing and gnashing of teeth. Already full and complete, they have no room to receive.

The incarnation of Jesus does not inaugurate a spiritual competition with rewards for right belief. Jesus issues an invitation to come and see, and his life shows us a way to seek the Lord and live while also sustaining us on that way. We seek because God hides.

And look, you may not like or approve of this aspect of God. Were I designing my god, I would channel Barbara Eden (look her up—or substitute Janet from *The Good Place*). I'd sculpt a hybrid cosmic bellhop, voice-activated, ever present and precisely responsive. Or, alternatively, a completely static god (perhaps like a stone or an ornately carved piece of metal) so I always knew exactly and only where to encounter (and how to avoid) the Holy One. But this is not who or how God is, and God has always been upfront about her sacred inscrutability. When Moses demanded to know God's name, God replied "I Will Be Who I Will Be."

We can't say we weren't warned.

The reasonable and perhaps universal response to all this is Why? Why does a God who supposedly loves us always hide from us? That, along with how many angels can dance on the top of the head of a pin, is a good and appropriate question but not one I have the capacity or the interest in answering. This is not a systematic theology. I don't know why God hides. If you don't like that part of God, sit down next to me, but don't ask me to do apologetics.

But after years of wrestling with the word of God and pastoring people, I know it to be true. God hides—and always in the people and places I least want to experience or explore. The thing is, as my very first childhood pastor Rev. James Chatham pointed out in his charge to me when I was ordained to ministry, nobody needs help finding God in the sunrise on the mountaintop, or in the first cry of their newborn child, or in the pathologist's report that the tumor is benign and no further treatment is needed. Even atheists acknowledge the holy in such moments. But a life of faith also finds God awesome and fully present in the storm, in the last breath of a beloved one, in the terminal diagnosis. God is present with us, to us, in all the parts of our lives that we initially sought God to avoid.

We, like the first disciples, hoped that if we followed Jesus, nothing bad would ever happen to us again. When Jesus reveals that the road ahead includes rejection, injustice, suffering, betrayal, and death, we too, drunk on fear and intimacy, stamp our feet with our big brother Peter and say, "Never Lord, I will not allow it." Jesus's warning to Peter, then, is for us too. It is Satan who appears as an angel of light, luring us with a religion that guarantees that nothing bad will ever happen to us again, and we will get whatever our heart desires.

Jesus never promises that nothing terrible will happen. He promises that he will be with us. Always. He leads us into the terror. He makes life with and for us even there, even on the cross, even from the grave. This is the glorious mystery.

We are eager to seek God in triumph, in blessing, in our dreams come true. And we find God there, sometimes. If your life is whole and unblemished, then what I'm going to say next seems like bad news.

But if you have suffered deeply and still carry the unhealed wounds, if you have lost what you couldn't bear to lose, if you want to punch the people who say God won't give you more than you can handle, if you are stuck in a life that you did everything you could to fix or avoid, then hear the good news: God hides in all the places and circumstances we are desperate to avoid. We all hope and believe that God won't let the terrible things that happen to other people happen to us. But we *are* other people. When we find ourselves in the situations we prayed God would deliver us from, we can also find God there. The truth is, our blessings and triumphs don't really show us the goodness of God. The awe-filled reality is that we learn the true depth of God's goodness in our grief, our failures, and our losses. We don't have to choose suffering. But when it comes to us anyway, we can choose to seek the God hidden within it. Seeking God's presence in our grief and loss does *not* require believing that God caused or is pleased by our pain. Seeking an explanation is different from seeking God.

There are a few ancient, well-worn spiritual paths we can follow if we wish to seek the hidden Christ. We look to these paths in the next three chapters. The first path is the practice of looking soberly at the ways our own choices are destructive and disordered. The second is the practice of releasing our desire for control of our own lives and other peoples. These practices have names: repentance and surrender.

To modern sensibilities, repentance and surrender seem like the warning signs you see outside abandoned mine shafts. Surely if there ever was anything good to discover down there, none of it remains now. Surely only repressed and gullible people ever found the Holy One through the spiritual practices of repentance and surrender, we "moderns" think. Now that we have therapists and pills, who needs such arcane practices anymore?

And if the words *repentance* and *surrender* didn't send you running for the hills, God's third favorite hiding place surely will: failure. God hides in our biggest losses and tragedies, the very ones we pray and work like anything to avoid.

It is because we are sure we've outgrown them that the practices of repentance and surrender make such lovely hiding spots for the Beloved. It is because we are certain nothing good can come from failing the One who is faithful to us in all seasons is certain to be found in our losses. Once we begin to understand that we have, as the poet Gerard Manley Hopkins said, a "Christ [who] plays in ten thousand places, / Lovely in limbs, and lovely in eyes not his," we must at least contemplate seeking him in exactly the places we don't expect to find him. Our God is good at hiding.

6

REPENTANCE

It's Not What You Think

DURING SEMINARY I had the great privilege of studying with author, humanitarian, Nobel Prize laureate, and Holocaust survivor Dr. Eliezer "Elie" Wiesel. I learned so much from him about how to live as a person of faith, about the destructive powers of totalitarianism and fascism, and about the transformational power of healthy communities and the disasters that occur in their absence. I also learned a lot about literature. He was the best teacher I've ever had.

One of the things Wiesel said that will never stop bothering me is that the first sentence is the most important part of any piece of writing. The first words must contain the whole world you are sharing. I find this both to be true and the source of 97 percent of all my procrastination.

Since I believe this is true, I find the first words of Jesus's public ministry troubling. If I were writing Jesus's marketing copy, I'd make his first word be "Love" or "Rejoice" or "Peace!" I'd have him echo the angels and say, "Fear not!" or "Good news!" Arguably, he needed an arresting phrase that would grab attention, so he could have gone with "Behold!" or "Wake Up!" or even "Watch Out!"

But none of these words are in Jesus's first recorded sentence. In the Gospel of Mark, Jesus's first sentence is one word. An imperative command. And it is the last word I ever want to use or hear. Jesus's first recorded word is "Repent."

For most of my life, I've wished it wasn't. I've learned the word *repent* is a threat. People scream at you to repent as they stand in judgment against you. It is both a warning and an indictment. This one word says, "I see you completely. I see who you are, and who you should be. I see through all your excuses and extenuating circumstances, and I demand that you do better. I require you to be other than you are, immediately."

In most people's mouths, the word *repent* is the moral equivalent of an *American Gladiators* challenge: a task possibly possible for the elite and über committed but practically impossible for the rest of us. Repent—but you can't and you won't. So functionally, the word *repent* becomes a demand that you back away slowly from the Holy One. There is no desire and no room for your kind around here. Come back when you are someone else.

I bear my own scars from the word *repent*, although they are minor compared to the wounds borne by many of my siblings in Christ. As a cisgender, heterosexual, white woman, I know my wounds are minuscule compared to the open wounds still carried by those who have been driven away. If the word *repent* carries no connotations of rejection and despair for you, you might believe that people who resist it are simply full of pride and willfulness, simply unwilling to look soberly and seriously at the brokenness of their own lives. But many people who run when they hear that word are actually following the Holy Spirit's command to flee. For them, the word *repent* was the catalyst of their spiritual trauma. When that word was hurled at them, it was not a call to reexamine their moral choices but to reject their own sacred selves. They were told to repent not of their actions but of their own sacred image, to reject their own souls to find union with God. And some loved the Lord so deeply and purely that for a long, long time they tried to hate themselves into God's embrace. They tried until the spirit of God came and gently pried their palms away from the hot iron of self-hatred and led them out of the church into the wilderness, where, like Jesus, they were attended by wild beasts and angels.

I am not ashamed of the gospel. But I am deeply grieved by the sacrilegious ways its raw power has been harnessed by the antichrist to steal, kill, lie, and wound humans created in the image of Christ. The power of the gospel was desecrated to justify chattel slavery, Jim Crow, and systemic racism. The power of the name of Jesus has been twisted to sanctify the genocide of Native Americans and the theft of both their land and their children. And the power of the gospel's clarion call to repentance was blasphemed when it was twisted to separate queer people from their own sacred souls. I hold space for the oceans of trauma unleashed on vulnerable people through the demonic weaponization of the word *repent.* I honor and respect the instinct to remove the word from our sacred vocabularies. The word has done so much damage. It is an ungodly irony that the word calling us away from suffering and destruction has unleashed so very, very much of it. To be deeply suspicious of people calling other people to repentance is exactly the kind of biblical shrewdness that Jesus celebrated.

And still. Jesus starts his ministry with this word. What do we do with that?

Many, many pastors have committed spiritual malpractice against LGBTQIA+ people. They have, knowingly and unknowingly, tortured humans seeking union with God. They have divided mothers from daughters and fathers from sons and driven people, not only out of the church, but also to take their own lives. In demonizing the identity of others, they have desecrated their own identity as pastors. But they do not have the power to desecrate the gospel or to destroy the whole practice of repentance.

If Jesus's call to repent, like so many other words in Jesus's mouth, does not mean what so many of us have been taught that it means, then what does it mean? What is Jesus calling us to?

* * *

Repentance is not a call to set aside the expression of our sacred identities and conform more closely to the patterns of this destructive culture. Instead, repentance is an invitation to turn around on our self-annihilating death march and begin walking and living in an entirely new way. It is the first step in a new way of living that seems like weakness and foolishness and failure but that inconceivably leads us into living our fullest, freest lives. I believe repentance is the path that leads us to where God is hiding in our own brokenness, waiting to be found to restore us to wholeness.

Jesus's call to repent, the invitation to be born again, is not a threat after all but a gift—a chance to become the most authentic versions of ourselves, to be born again as the people we were created to be. When Jesus calls people to repent, the call is especially for those who believe they are the closest to God.

It's okay if you're not buying any of this.

I get it. I have never felt, before or since, the kind of rage I felt the first time someone called me personally to repent. It took everything in me not to stand up on my chair and shout, "Who the *hell* do you think you are?"

It happened during the first gathering of the group of ten pastors whose churches were chosen to participate in the pilot of the transformation journey designed by our presbytery. We all applied to be in the project, answering the call of our local denominational leader for pastors who believed that their churches needed deep change in order to survive. The whole thing was explicitly designed for congregations that recognized that if they continued in their settled patterns, they would die. I signed up to be part of this process, filled out an application, and wrote multiple essays about why we would be a good fit. I prayed we would be accepted.

Still, when on the first day a consultant standing in a pulpit told me that our churches were dying because we had been unfaithful and that I personally would have to repent, I was deeply, deeply offended. I had shown up to be encouraged. I was there to be affirmed. I came to be resourced. All those things were waiting for me, as well as a wild and glorious renewal beyond anything I could have hoped or imagined. But the first step, unwelcome and deeply insulting, was a call to repent.

I was offended, because I did not understand what repentance meant. I thought it was a call to despise who I was and renounce God's call on my life. I was offended because I misunderstood the sacred universality of repentance. The call to repent is an urgent invitation to reconsider faith and practice. The more seriously we take our faith, the more open we are to repentance. That day, the call to repent was an invitation to pause and open myself up to unlearning, to deep questioning, and to examining not just what wasn't working in my eyes, but also what I was quite certain *was* working. I was offended because I wasn't ready for it.

I came ready to go all in that first day of the transformation project. I came with a notebook and pen to write everything down. I showed up ready to work hard and get serious. But I was not there to be changed. The only thing I knew for sure was that *I* was not the problem. I expected the Lord would equip me with strategies to unlock other people's full potential. (Strategies they should have taught me in seminary!) I wondered if God might empower me to prophetically call the congregation out of apathy into the kind of action I was already taking. Privately, I suspected that the transformation project was designed to help others level up to the kind of commitment I already had. I had all sorts of secret hopes and expectations about what transformation might look like.

But it literally never occurred to me that it would change me. It was inconceivable to me that the change I sought had anything to do with me, personally. I honestly thought that everything needed to change *except* me. I wasn't foolish enough to say it out loud, but I was sure I only had the acceptable "virtues disguised as faults." You know, the ones you cop out on when they make you name your weaknesses in job interviews: "I tend to work too hard. I really care too much."

I mean, what had repentance to do with me?

All these years later, I have tenderness toward the young woman I was. I was so sincerely committed to earning my righteousness. But still, it astonishes me how little a lifetime of churchgoing, four years of graduate-level theological education, and a decade of employment as a pastor had prepared me to hear the word *repent*. For sure, I had ego issues. But it wasn't even that I believed I was that extraordinary. The call to repentance was inconceivable to me because I did not think I could be in need of repentance and still belong to Jesus. My faith in Jesus and work for Jesus were so deeply intertwined, and my identity as a pastor and my experience of God's acceptance of me were so enmeshed, that a call to repent was an ontological threat. How could God love and accept me if I needed to change? If I needed to repent, did that mean that everything about my life and self-understanding was a lie? And the deeper, hidden question: Would I still love God if God wanted to do more than affirm me? Would I still want God if God wanted to make me new?

The call to repentance is not a call to conform more deeply to the world's expectations of us but to cast them off. Repentance interrupts our self-soothing, our confidence that we are good Christians who do not need to grow or change. In our age, the call to repentance is a call to quit fighting the culture wars, quit congratulating ourselves on the degrees and honors we've achieved, and quit celebrating ego-driven burnout. It's a call to recalibrate our moral compass to the Sermon on the Mount. The call to repent is an invitation to place on the altar not only the parts of life that we see as wretched but also the parts of life that we cling to. To repent is to pray with the psalmist: "Search me, God, and know my heart; test me and know my anxious thoughts. See if there is any offensive way in me, and lead me in the way everlasting" (Ps 139:23–24). The call to repentance is not a test or a trap, but an invitation to trust that God has even more life for you. It is an invitation to unclench your fists and see what falls from your open relaxed hand. A call to look around and see what might be manna—strange and unfamiliar blessings that nourish us, even the very bread of angels. Repentance is the path from certainty to uncertainty, which is to say, the path to faith.

It is a call, not a demand. But make no mistake, it is a call to wonder what might be wrong not in others but in yourself. It is a willingness to learn from the One who made you and sustains you in love. It is an eagerness to hear how you have lost the path and forsaken parts of your own blessing.

In his Sermon on the Mount, Jesus asks us how we plan to take the speck out of our brother's eye when there's a log in our own. Often, with diabolical irony, those who are the most committed to the work of justice and liberation are the most resistant to the spiritual practice of repentance. We see so clearly what is wrong with other people and somehow we conclude that the depravity of the "other" is proof of our own sanctity. If my neighbor or my enemy has so very much to repent of, surely that means that there is no real need for *me* to repent.

* * *

For generations, Black American spiritual leaders have been naming the destructive power of Christians believing they are too righteous to repent. Dr. King famously concluded that the greatest stumbling block before the movement was not "the White Citizen's Councilor or the Ku Klux Klanner, but the white moderate." White moderates during that time believed that righteousness only demanded that they refrain from violently assaulting and directly threatening Black Americans. They were unwilling to see that passively standing by without challenging or disrupting the status quo propped up racist systems. King called them to repentance because they were "more devoted to 'order' than to justice . . . and 'prefer a negative peace which is the absence of tension to a positive peace which is the presence of justice' . . . [they] constantly say: 'I agree with you in the goal that you seek, but I cannot agree with your methods of direct action.'" It was King's pastoral call for his allies, as well as his enemies, to repent that made him the most hated man in America at the time of his murder.

One of the greatest places of consensus among Black justice advocates today is a shared experience of vicious hostility and opposition among white allies when they are called to repent. One of evil's most effective moves is to convince us that if we self-identify as allies, we have no need to learn, no need to change, no faults to correct, no damage to atone for.

My father's law firm had several cases that involved the Walmart corporation. He had to travel to their headquarters in Bentonville, Arkansas, more than once. He told me that there was a big sign over the door leading to the legal offices that said WDWDW? He asked them what it stood for and they told him it meant "What Did We Do Wrong?" I wonder how much healthier and holier churches would be if we hung similar signs over our sanctuary doors. I wonder how much more loving we Christians would be if we wore bracelets asking ourselves to reflect upon WDWDW instead of WWJD.

One of the extraordinarily rare pieces of cultural consensus right now is that there is a lot wrong. And we are all experts in how other people are the cause of almost all of it. We would happily and clearly tell our neighbors and enemies and family members what they do wrong, if they would only listen. But we have no interest in learning what we have done wrong. We'll tell almost anyone what's wrong with them. We'll put it in a TikTok or a PowerPoint presentation. But we are terrified to genuinely ask the question: What's wrong with me? According to my dad's story, the Walmart corporation is more open to repentance than the average American Christian.

Some of us are so confident in God's love for us, so confident that we are good and loving people, that we no longer care to discover how we might be contributing to the suffering of our siblings. Some of us are so glad that grace gives us freedom to live without fearing God's wrath that we are no longer interested in sincerely discovering how God might be inviting us to live differently. If you ask any non-narcissist follower of Jesus the question, "Are you perfect?" they will be vehement in their denial. All of us acknowledge that we are sinners. Many of us admit in our weekly Sunday liturgy that we sin against God and our neighbors "by what we have done and what we have left undone," as the Book of Common Prayer says. But we don't want to know what we've done wrong.

Maybe it's not safe or sane to ask your enemy or your neighbor or your mother what's wrong with you. But we all need communities where it *is* safe to ask that question. And the witness of Scripture is clear: It is not only safe but life-giving to ask Jesus what we have done wrong. It's not just good; it's an imperative. If confidence in God's love for us makes us callous to the suffering of others and uninterested in the ways we may be causing harm, then we are in danger of becoming moral monsters.

* * *

People in recovery are some of our best spiritual teachers about repentance. They have courageously faced the question, "What's wrong with me?" And they have heard the answer: "Your addiction is destroying your life." They admit life as it is is no longer manageable, even though they do not yet know any other way. That's repentance. It flourishes in recovery communities because it is honored there. It is safe to repent at an AA meeting. It's safe to tell what you have done wrong. You won't be attacked or judged or shamed. You will be celebrated for no longer denying your weakness. You will be supported and guided as you seek healing and new paths and in the process of making amends.

I believe that one of the reasons that white supremacy is so entrenched in the United States is that white people refuse to learn what we've done wrong. We will not confront the truth of the harm white supremacist ideologies continue to cause, and we refuse to listen when anyone generously offers to show us how deeply this culture has been embedded in our individual and collective consciousness. We think: Whatever is wrong, it couldn't be me. I have nothing to repent of, and even if I did, there's no point. Nothing about my life needs to change. Enough of your lived experience; and stop sharing your pain; it's making me feel bad!

Christians reclaiming the spiritual practice of repentance could be a tremendous source of healing and renewal in the world. Imagine what might grow out of spaces where it is safe and holy to wonder "What did I do wrong?"; where it is considered an act of love to reverently listen when someone tells you the truth, even when it doesn't flatter you; where there is a deep trust that healing change can happen and people are more than their worst choices and biggest mistakes.

Years ago, I got in trouble when I arranged for an adult, summer Sunday school class to write letters of support to people in prison. An angry elder cornered me afterward. "I don't come to church to make criminals feel good about themselves! They shouldn't feel good; they're there for a reason. I'm sick of hearing about inmates discovering Jesus on death row; they're only Christians now because they hope it will save their lives."

But the truth is, we're all on death row. And we're all following Jesus because we hope he will save our lives. Jesus's first word to all of us is "Repent!" Repentance should be centered and celebrated in Christian churches, because *we all* are the people who need it.

God hides in our brokenness, in our weakness, in our moral failures. God hides in our need for forgiveness and healing and change, and these are exactly the places where repentance leads us. Repentance uncovers our deep existential need and vulnerability. We fear repentance because we believe it will lead God to reject and condemn us the way we reject and condemn one another. We don't want to go there.

So it is precisely there that we will encounter God. And when we do, we will be relieved to discover that God is God, and we are not. Our way of dealing with the brokenness of the world is not God's way. Repentance is asking the God who made us, "How do I need to change? What are you calling me away from? What are you calling me toward? What have I done wrong?" Most importantly, it is asking "Will you help me?" When we are safe and brave enough to ask those questions, God will meet us in the answers. If we refuse to seek God in those questions, we will never fully know the tenderness and transformation of the love of God.

7

SURRENDER

I Might Not Get What I Want

IN THE DAYS before the beltway that loops Charlotte was completed, I had a very long commute to the church. Those were the days after everything had fallen apart but before any signs of new life could be seen, and it felt like I spent half my life sitting in stoplights on Harris Boulevard. In those days, when the work seemed never ending and futile, I wore my exhaustion like spiritual armor, and my endless, fruitless effort was my proudest accomplishment. Nothing was working, but no one could accuse me of not trying. Nothing was working, but no one could convict me of being okay with it. Nothing was working, but at least I was miserable about it.

I was so full of anxiety and stress and distraction that it was only when I was trapped in my car on my commute that God could get my undivided, resentful attention. One Monday morning sitting in traffic, on my way to the church, I had what I can only describe as a mystical encounter.

It was the beginning of the week, the beginning of my day, the beginning of my commute, and already I was so behind and so exhausted. My eyes drifted up, and I noticed some huge hawks above me. I watched as one took off from a utility pole, pumping its wings vigorously for several seconds and flying straight upward until it caught an air current. Then the hawk spread its wings and began to glide. I kept watching the hawks. Each flight began with a few seconds of vigorous pumping, and then came the glide—moments of stretched-out stillness, effortless riding on the invisible wind.

It made me so angry.

The sight of those birds bursting into flight and then gracefully gliding pierced my soul. Why did it feel like all I ever did was pump and pump and pump as strongly and as furiously as I could just to save myself from free fall? Why did I never get to glide?

That moment fractured my spiritual foundation. I felt the Lord saying to me, "There is another way, a way where the yoke is easy, and the burden is light. Consider the birds, literally. You could have the glide; you could be in this life resting on and being held by the Holy Spirit and not your own furious efforts. But to get there, you'll have to forsake all your striving, all your performing, all your demands and expectations and, most importantly, all your ferocious attempts to make your own path. To get there, you'll have to go where the wind is taking you."

Watching those hawks opened a tiny, almost imperceptible fissure in my settled understanding of the sacred. An unfamiliar part of my heart experienced the invitation to let go like water poured on parched ground, like a cell door swinging open. But to the vast majority of my heart, that invitation felt like a death sentence. It felt like giving up. It seemed like Jack letting go of the door at the end of *Titanic*. Just let go? Just give up? This was indulgent, spiritualized laziness, and it would lead not to flying but crashing. I turned on NPR and went back to righteously worrying about the world.

At my church, we often sing a song about moving from an intellectual faith to an embodied one, moving out of our heads and into our hearts. In the song, we give the Spirit permission to lead us on a journey, past our certainties and desires, until we are lost in God. I wasn't aware of it or aware that I needed it, but in that season, the Lord was pulling and prying me out of my head and into my heart, into an unwelcome awareness of my body, into a disorienting contemplation of my daily choices. Jesus was inviting me to trade productivity for presence. And I was resisting.

I was committed to earnestly and ceaselessly striving to perform, to please God with my plans. I loved Jesus, and I wanted to work for him. But Jesus didn't invite anybody to come and work for him. The invitation, ever and always, is "come and see, come and follow." I didn't want to see, and I didn't want to follow. I wanted to do, and I wanted to lead. I wanted my faith to be productive. I was certain I knew what that could and should look like. A pastor friend used to wear an ironic T-shirt that said, "Jesus Is Coming. Look Busy!" I didn't understand why it was funny.

In those days, I talked the talk. I preached sermons about trusting God, about walking by faith and not by sight, about leaning not on our own understanding. I preached sermons about Jesus calming the storm, sermons inviting people to trust that God would help them when they couldn't help themselves. I taught about Jesus multiplying the loaves and fishes and asked people to not just trust Jesus with the little that they had but to trust him expectantly, waiting on him to magnify what was small and insignificant and make it more than it was. I preached Jesus-casting-out-demons sermons and promised people that when they couldn't try any harder to be good, to get free, to turn their lives around, Jesus's love would release them and free them from the demons of addiction or hate or greed or late capitalism or whatever was binding them. I encouraged other people to trust Jesus, to be like those hawks launching themselves out into the unknown, knowing an air current would catch them and they would glide. I preached those sermons, and I meant them—for other people.

My life and my ministry (which were pretty much the same in those days) weren't grounded in trusting Jesus, much less surrendering my action plans. Instead, I trusted my good ideas and Jesus's ability to bring them to completion. I preached sermons on faith, but I didn't really have any. Instead of faith, I had determination. I had the conviction that if I could just get everyone else on board, Jesus working through me would make everything okay in my eyes. I had plans. I had degrees. I had a Reformed Protestant work ethic. I had good intentions and right understanding and social capital. I believed all those things came from Jesus, and I trusted in them. I believed that Jesus had given me all those assets and expected me to leverage them for the kingdom.

It's not what we say or think or agree with that reveals what we believe but how we live. And I wasn't interested in a faith that required me to trust Jesus and surrender. I signed on for a life of getting work done for Christ. I was committed to pumping my wings for all eternity. Functionally, I was an atheist.

I was unaware of it, but I actually had an anti-faith internal operating system. I had a script of assumptions that undergirded all my awareness of the world, all my choices, all my loving and seeing and serving. I trusted Jesus to make my plans work out and my good choices pay off. I believed with all my heart and soul that if I just kept showing up and working hard and doing my best and sharing my gifts, God would use my efforts to calm metaphorical storms, multiply gifts, and heal and restore people. I'd worked hard to study and learn and plan and serve. All my degrees and certifications and ordination exams had revealed me to be more than adequate. I earnestly believed that Jesus was at work in the world, healing, blessing, consoling, and sustaining. And I thought he was doing all those things through the earnest, diligent efforts of people like me.

It's deeply embarrassing to confess this now. Of course, I would have angrily denied all of this at the time had anyone suggested it. But while I trusted Jesus with eternity, my unconscious expectation was that in this life, Jesus was depending on people like me to build his kingdom. Regardless of what I preached on a Sunday, I operated as if Jesus had made a good start on the cross and then left all of us to finish the job on his behalf.

Which is why I couldn't stop striving, couldn't stop hustling, couldn't stop scheming and working and going to meetings and writing emails and planning programs and attending conferences and listening to podcasts and reading books and pumping my wings as hard as I could against the headwinds, because my heart believed that I was all there was. My heart was sure that if I stopped, I would fall—and maybe even take Jesus down with me. My heart was certain that there was nothing—no one—to catch me, much less help me glide.

* * *

In those days, my friends were a saving grace. I used to meet my friend Eustacia for lunch almost every Thursday, and we'd talk about worship and preaching and church renewal. One day, I started sharing with her my master plan for revitalizing the congregation. It hinged upon our winning a grant that our denomination offered to churches with promising outreach prospects. The five-year grant paid the pastor's full salary for the first year, then 80 percent the second year, and 60 percent the third year, and so on until the church was thriving and self-sufficient. The first congregation where I was ordained and served as an associate pastor had qualified for one of those grants in the early 1990s, and now it was stable and thriving. I was sure the grant was the key for that church, and that it would make all the difference in this current church as well. All I had to do was show the denominational executives that this congregation in this city was worthy.

Eustacia listened to me and then, with extraordinary tenderness, delivered one of the most succinct calls to repentance I've ever heard: "If you are counting on the Presbytery to save you, you are in big trouble."

She went on to explain that the denomination had ended that program, to which I replied, well, we'd just have to bring it back because it was effective. Like a true friend, she loved me enough to tell me the truth, knowing that I couldn't yet see or accept it. Hearing that the grant program I'd built my plans upon wasn't available anymore felt like a death blow. Because if we'd gotten the grant, I would have sincerely given all the credit for our revival to Jesus, but now that I knew we wouldn't be getting it, I couldn't see another path to saving the church. It never occurred to me that Jesus alone could still save us, even without a grant. It never occurred to me that God might be hiding in this dead end, waiting to provide.

Again, it pains me to acknowledge this now, but my unconscious assumption was that Jesus was at work in the world through the systems and the institutions of the world. Churches would be revitalized by Jesus, sure, but *through* their denominations. People would receive justice from Jesus through the criminal justice system. Jesus protected people through the military and the police. Jesus helped the poor through charities and philanthropy. Jesus established order through civic governments, healed people through health care systems, and created abundance through the stock market. I knew that these systems and institutions were unjust and needed renewal and repair, but I functioned in ministry as though they were the primary channels through which Jesus worked. I knew these systems were flawed and unfaithful, but I believed that Jesus had called and anointed people like me, for such a time as this, to redeem them.

Of course, I believed this. I was a young, privileged white woman. All the systems I implicitly trusted had worked for me and people who looked like me. And that day, in the salad bar, when Eustacia told me that the grant I was counting on had ended and that I couldn't count on denominational institutions to save me, it felt like she was telling me there was no hope. I still believed in Jesus, but How could *he* help me if the denomination wouldn't?

Eustacia wasn't telling me to give up hope; she was telling me to hope in Jesus and not human institutions. But in that season of my life, being told to trust in Jesus felt like a prescription for hospice care, the thing you say to someone when death is inevitable, to get them to hold it together so you don't have to witness the breakdown. "Hope in Jesus" is the way people tell you to give up the fight and get out of the way. You are about to lose everything you care about—but *trust Jesus*: he will make the process as painless and comfortable as possible. I saw *trust Jesus* as a spiritual euphemism for passive resignation, and I didn't want to give up. I didn't want to fail. I didn't want the church to die.

So I hatched new plans. National grants, partnering with nonprofits, renting parts of our building, nesting a foster home, yoking with a larger local congregation. I conceived each plan after hours of research and dozens of coffee and lunch meetings. Some of them fizzled out almost immediately, some of them blew up in the middle stages, and one gloriously imploded on the very last day, leaving me struggling not to cry around a board table in front of kind men in suits.

My Hail Mary was a gospel concert on the lawn. One summer evening of joy, guest musicians from all over the city, attracting neighbors and friends and strangers. They would come and be filled with joy and the Spirit and see this beautiful community and decide it was too good to die. A concert! That was the ticket. A gospel concert, with a homemade program where everyone bought "ads" to support us: That would save us! Somehow, it would be the small thing that became the catalyst for a great big transformation. It would be the spiritual domino that triggered an unlikely chain reaction that unleashed flourishing in the people and the place that everyone had given up.

A concert—the wacky last-ditch effort of every save-the-camp, school, theater, farm, town Disney (or Hallmark) movie ever made.

It would work because it had to. Because this church could be so beautiful, could be so real and healthy and transformative. It would work, because this community was such a unique and essential expression of the kingdom of God. And some day, when people asked me how the church had so improbably lived and not died, first, I'd say Jesus. And then, after we'd all agreed it was nothing but the Lord, I'd tell them about how I'd almost given up but then I decided to try one last thing. I'd tell them about a gospel concert on a steamy Thursday evening in August, and about how that spectacular night was the beginning of not-the-end of us.

* * *

Concert planning commenced. Another plan piled on all the other plans. Inviting, marketing, explaining, cajoling. It was frantic faithfulness. I was already planning sermons and Bible studies, I was already planning a capital campaign and a summer Vacation Bible School, I was already planning an end-of-camp Sunday morning celebration and a revitalization of our after-school program to roll out in the fall, and—not that it counted as faithfulness in my sight at that time—but I was also planning birthday parties for my summer-born daughters. So what was it to plan one more thing? I didn't know any other way to follow Jesus but to feverishly pump my wings. I was Icarus in leggings and a messy mom bun, except I never got to touch the sun. I wasn't naive. I knew how unlikely it was that this concert would change everything, but I just wasn't ready to give up.

And then, five days before the concert, the watermelon sitting on my kitchen counter spontaneously combusted.

I know it's unbelievable, but it's a thing. Google it. It doesn't happen often, but it happened to me that summer. I woke up on Saturday morning to the sound of my husband screaming my name from the kitchen, and when I ran in, it was everywhere. Slimy, red worms of putrid watermelon, on the ceiling, on the walls, on the floor, all over the dishes, on the open shelves, in the drawers—everywhere.

And the smell. Dear God, the smell.

The smell of fermented watermelon is truly indescribable, but it resembles a child's vomit at the end of a birthday party, except stronger and sweeter. Did I mention it was everywhere?

It took both of us four hours to clean it up, the whole time breathing in that smell on our empty stomachs. And even after all that, for weeks I kept finding strands of it in corners and crevices, hidden from sight but still pungent. And this was the room where I prepared food. It was horrible. And I had no choice but to add "scour every inch and crevice of our kitchen" to my groaning to-do list.

Later that day, I sat down with my spiritual director. I was there to get counsel, of course, but also to share my vision for the "gospel concert that would save the church" plan. I planned to tell her with such charm and passion that she would spontaneously decide to join in *and* offer to lead an opening prayer *and* invite her other pastor friends *and* their churches to participate. I took a deep breath and opened my mouth and a sob came out.

All I could do was cry. About the discontinued grant, and the leaking roof, and my humiliation at the boardroom table, and the members who were leaving, and the newcomers who weren't coming, and hawks that got to glide while I had to just work and worry as hard as I could until I crashed, failing to execute all the plans I couldn't pull off but couldn't let go of, and about the damn exploding watermelon that just pushed me over the edge.

Because here I was, down here, doing all the trying harder and harder, all the not giving up. And meanwhile, Jesus was exploding fermenting fruit on my kitchen counter.

My spiritual director just looked at me and said, "Aren't you tired?"

And I didn't even know how to answer that question. Because why did it matter? Because wasn't everyone? Because wasn't that the point, to pour yourself out like a drink offering before the Lord?

As I opened my mouth to brush off the question, revelation struck in the way it does, when your mind grasps something for the first time and finally catches up to what your body and spirit have known for ages: I. Was. The. Watermelon.

In retrospect, I am quite sure that my vision of a save-the-church community gospel concert didn't come from the Lord but from the unholy union of my ego and anxiety. But when I ignored the sign of the hawks gliding above me as I was stuck in traffic, Jesus gave me a parable that I couldn't ignore: The Sign of the Exploding Watermelon. My plans and striving, my not giving up and trying harder—all of it was pressure cooking me from the inside out. I didn't want to change. I didn't know any other way to be. But in that moment, I understood that I couldn't go on as I was, not if it meant destroying myself and exploding on everyone I loved. I couldn't give up, but I couldn't go on, and in my mind, those were my only choices.

When she saw I wouldn't answer the question, my spiritual director just looked at me and said, "You know, it really doesn't have to be like this."

My spiritual director had talked to me about surrender, often. But that was the first time I was sad and tired and scared enough to consider actually doing it. For the first time in my life, I wondered about surrender. Maybe it was more than a metaphor for being humble. Maybe surrender wasn't a "one and done" thing that pastors screamed about at revivals to manipulate people into joining institutions. Maybe it wasn't just a spiritualized way of justifying it when you give up and stop trying.

I allowed myself to consider that my expectations and anxiety and certainty had become unbearable burdens. Maybe they weren't necessary or useful motivational tools. Maybe they were the bars that trapped me in the prison of myself. Maybe they were poisons that blinded me to where God was in my life. Maybe they were walls separating me from the people I loved and sincerely wanted to serve.

Maybe they were the idols I put my trust in more than Christ.

When you put it out there like this, it seems self-help-like easy. Of course, let go of your stupid plans that don't work out anyway, and trust Jesus. But as awful as my plans and expectations and assumptions were, they promised to get me to where I wanted to go. Even when I knew they were futile, my plans and effort gave me the illusion of control. And even when you know it's fake, the illusion of control is painful to lose. It never becomes comfortable to feel like you are not in control, but at first it feels like you're dying. At first, it feels like free fall.

I was certainly no expert in surrendering. All I knew is that it meant that Jesus got to call the shots and choose the paths. And the dumb, embarrassing truth is I wasn't sure that I trusted him. It's one thing to turn to Jesus trusting that, by his grace, you will receive everything you want most. It's another thing entirely to turn to Jesus and trust that, by his grace, you will become everything that he wants most. I knew Jesus well enough to strongly suspect that *my* idea of my best life and *his* idea of my best life were not the same. I wanted to serve Jesus, but I wasn't sure I wanted to be the kind of believer who surrendered, who trusted Jesus no matter what.

What I'm saying is I wasn't trying to find Christian nirvana in a hazelnut. Because now that I've told you about the watermelon, I need to tell you about the hazelnut.

* * *

Julian of Norwich was born around 1343 and died in 1416. She was a mystic, which is already suspicious enough, but she was also an anchoress. Anchorites were the ultramarathoners of monastics. Like all monastics, they voluntarily withdrew from the secular world and chose a life of perpetual prayer and meditation. But unlike typical monastics, they committed to a life of sedentary solitude. Alone, in one monastic cell, forever, like voluntary spiritual solitary confinement. I'm not saying there's anything wrong with that kind of spirituality; I'm just saying I don't want any part of it.

Anchorites entered their confinement with a religious rite called a consecration, which borrowed the liturgy of the funeral mass, because from that point on they were considered living saints. They were believers who died completely to their previous lives. As part of the rite, they took a vow of permanent stability. Like, a "stay put even if the building's on fire" kind of stability. They stepped into a room and the door was bricked up behind them. They were literally entombed by their sacred vows.

Not many men became anchorites; it was kind of a chick thing, perhaps because even in their sealed, shut cells, anchoresses had more authority, autonomy, and freedom than women living secular or more typical religious lives. Because she was an anchorite, Julian was also allowed to be a theologian and a poet. Her "living saint" status meant that her writings were collected, preserved, and eventually published in a book called *Revelations of Divine Love*. This is the earliest known literary work in the English language by a woman.

But Julian's life in her ten-by-ten-foot cell with a chamber pot wasn't all freedom and good times. Her faith was shaped by disease, tragedy, and war. She was a young woman when the Black Death first rolled through Norwich and killed half the population. The plague returned several more times during her lifetime. She was surrounded by terror and destruction, yet her writing contains tender and beautiful descriptions of the maternal nature of God. Many scholars believe these images are drawn from her own experience as a mother; they speculate that she chose life as an anchoress after she lost her own family to the plague. Every year of her life happened during the Hundred Years' War between England and France. Even locked away in her cell, she wasn't safe when tensions within England sparked the Peasants' Revolt. Many of the battles in that civil war were fought in her own city.

Julian was a mystic, which means her knowledge of God came through direct, supernatural encounters. She took her vows in response to her first mystical vision, which came while she was dangerously ill. Believing she was close to death, her family sent for the priest. As he administered the last rites, she looked up and saw a vision of Jesus bleeding on the cross above her bed. This is pretty much exactly what I do not want to see, ever, but Julian made a miraculous full recovery, which she attributed to the healing power of her mystical vision. She went on to describe it as the first of her "shewings."

When you read about her life, the sickness, the loss of her children, plagues, revolutions, wars, solitary confinement in a ten-by-ten-foot cell with a cat, it sounds like one long unbroken chain of tragedies. You'd expect her to be the TULIPiest of Calvinists. But her theology is full of joy and hope and remarkable serenity. Through her writings, this woman, who had suffered unbearable loss, who lived within the most severe limits and under constant threat of death, and who found God hiding in all of it, reassures those seeking the sacred that "God is nearer to us than our own soul."

When people sought out her wisdom and peace, she encouraged them with visions of the tenderness of God's sovereignty, the most famous of which is Jesus singing to her like a lullaby: "All shall be well, and all shall be well, and all manner of things shall be well." You have to wonder what made her so confident. The plagues? The wars? The tragic loss of her family? The way she had to wall herself into a cell to achieve any measure of freedom or autonomy? How in the world did she become convinced that the future would be "well" when her past and present were so full of pain and suffering?

Her description of the way Jesus spoke to her in the "all shall be well" vision is also revelatory. She writes, "This was said so tenderly, without blame of any kind toward me or anybody else." What must her interior life with Jesus have been like that instead of protesting this revelation she savored it?

Talk about full surrender. Julian was a middle-aged woman living in the Middle Ages, entombed in a monastic cell. She was utterly vulnerable. When she stepped into that cell, she gave up all control. Her life with God wasn't a commodity she could sell or a power she could leverage to change her circumstances. Instead, it was a generative and joy-filled peace she rested in. From her confinement, she soared.

Julian of Norwich is perhaps most remembered for her description of the revelation Jesus gave to her "of a small thing, little as a hazelnut and round as a ball." She asked the Lord, "What can this be?" and heard him respond, "It is all that is."

From that vision of a hazelnut, Julian came to believe three things about God's relationship with all of creation: "God made it, God loves it and God keeps it." Chaos and violence raged around her, but within her cell, within herself, she found a dynamic and limitless life with Christ. She received the whole of John's revelation on Patmos in one vision of a hazelnut.

Julian is pretty much the antithesis of a Christian lifestyle influencer. So many influential leaders build large platforms and churches and followings these days, essentially by saying: "I love Jesus; look at my life, you can too!" Julian's life included everything we'd sell our souls to avoid: limits, loss, tragedy, vulnerability. And yet, inexplicably, from her cell she soaks in the infinite presence of God. Despite the precarity of the times, the misogyny and ignorance around her, and the literal physical limits of her life and culture, she leaves an indelible legacy. She speaks to us still, eight hundred years after her death. Her life seems to testify that people can both know they are made and loved and kept by God and experience God's belovedness neither in their circumstances nor despite their circumstances but regardless of them.

Julian writes that she sought to understand the meaning of God's first revelation to her of Christ suffering on the cross for many years and finally heard God's response:

> *You would know our Lord's meaning in this thing?*
> *Know it well.*
> *Love was His meaning.*
> *Who showed it to you? Love. What did He show you?*
> *Love.*
> *Why did He show it? For love.*
> *Hold on to this and you will know and understand love*
> *more and more.*
> *But you will not know or learn anything else—ever.*

It rhymes, theologically, with Paul's stumbling block claim that God makes all things work together for good for those who love the Lord (Rom 8:28). From my perspective, nothing in Julian's life was good. She lost her children, she surrendered her autonomy and freedom, and she lived under constant threat of violence and disease. I pray that God will protect me from everything that happened to Julian. Yet somehow, in the midst of it all, she was with Christ, and it was well with her soul. This is the promise of surrender: that God will be with us and all will be well, no matter what.

I am not reassured by the thought that all will be well no matter what. I want everything to be good, and the "what" matters to me. I want the gospel to promise me that since God is good, if I am good, my circumstances will be good. I want to be so protected from evil that it never even occurs to me to pray to be delivered from it. I want a life so steady and secure that when, as the psalmist notes, "A thousand fall at my side and 10,000 fall at my right hand, and it [does] not come near me," (Ps 91:7; my translation). I don't even notice, because it's just another ordinary Tuesday.

But all evil came near Julian. It doesn't seem that God delivered her from anything, and yet she found an abundant life right there in her little ten-by-ten-foot cell.

* * *

When they talk about surrender, television preachers lie. Televangelists say that if we surrender to Jesus, we will end up getting everything we want. They say if you surrender to God and buy their prayer cards, you will have total control. But Julian's mysticism reveals the real and unmarketable truth. Surrender is a moment of holy disillusionment. It strips away our desire to be in control, uncovering our terrifying vulnerability. Our surrender is a sacred acceptance that God is good, and we are loved, but we are not and never will be in control. Selah.

Before you are ready, surrender feels like death. But when you're ready, surrender feels like a relief. When you are ready, it turns out surrender isn't the free fall plunge to your death you were certain it would be. When you are ready, it turns out surrender is the glide.

Love drew me to Jesus. And love for him and the vision and promises of the kingdom led me to wholeheartedly embrace my call to ministry. But once I got deep into this life, once I got serious about Jesus and ministry, I pushed love to the sidelines. I had vital, important work to do. I had people to serve and injustices to right and churches to save. All this required serious, sustained effort. The stakes were so high, nothing could be left to chance—I mean, God. I needed total and complete control.

So God, for love's sake, disillusioned me. Control was the pressure or rot that exploded the watermelon. We cannot live with control.

It is an illusion that will destroy us. But we can live with love. Until we are satisfied by loving and being loved by God, we will never be free. Until loving and being loved is enough, we will never glide.

Our lives are so achingly fragile, and our power to protect ourselves and those we love is torturously limited. Surrender is accepting that everything terrible that happens to anyone happens to someone God loved into existence, so anything that happens can happen to you. Surrender is knowing that and then deciding that God is still beautiful to you. Surrender is Shadrach, Meshach, and Abednego, the faithful Hebrews condemned to death for refusing to worship and swear loyalty to imperial idols. In Daniel 3:16–18, they stand before the fiery furnace, defiantly bearing witness: "If we are thrown into the blazing furnace, the God we serve is able to deliver us from it, and he will deliver us from Your Majesty's hand. But even if he does not, we want you to know, Your Majesty, that we will not serve your gods or worship the image of gold you have set up."

Surrender is counting the cost and deciding that even if it doesn't work out, even if you don't prevail, even if the worst happens, you still want to align your heart with God's heart. It's pure, nontransactional love. It's the stunning realization that if what you want is not what God wants for you, then you don't want it anymore. It's the grace of realizing "thy will be done" is no longer just a line in a prayer but the authentic desire of your whole heart. It's the shift that comes when you realize that not being able to control the outcomes means you aren't responsible for controlling the outcomes. It's the strange peace you find when you discover the power of the words "there is nothing else I can do."

Ultimately, surrender is as simple and impossible as accepting that God is God and you are not and rejoicing in that fact. Somehow that revelation changes nothing and changes everything. That's the truth that allows you, with your last bit of strength, to spread your wings and soar while you wait for the wind to catch you.

8

FAILURE

We Will Lose. A Lot.

CELEBRITY PASTORS AND bestselling Christian authors proclaim that the power of God is made available to us so that we can triumph. A quick glance at the "Christian Living" section in the local bookstore makes this abundantly clear. Once we learn *The Secret*, we can *Dream Big*, because we know *Faith Still Moves Mountains*. We give our *Utmost for His Highest*. We're told to *Wash Your Face* and *Quit Apologizing*, so we can move from *Good to Great* and start *Winning on Purpose*. True faith will lead to victory: *Victory in Christ*, *Victory in Jesus*, *Victory over the Darkness*, *Victory in Prayer*, *Victory in Spiritual Warfare*, and *Our Ultimate Victory*. Because, after all, *Victory: Your Only Option*.

I've read and appreciated several of these books, but the cumulative message of the Christian industrial complex is inescapable: The power of God, rightly used, will make faithful people triumphant. That victory can look different—maybe it's spiritual peace, maybe it's physical healing, maybe it's success, or political power, or growth or influence or safety or public acclaim or financial security. But whatever it is, it's winning. Victory might be delayed, or it might manifest in an unexpected way, but it will not be denied. All our personal testimonies will end with yes and amen. There must be victory in Jesus. Otherwise, what's the point? (Also, how would we move merch?)

We turn to the gospel to behold the power of God, and we are taught by the experts that holy power will make us big, centered, and celebrated success stories. After all, *My Fame, His Fame.* Over and over, we hear that God gives us the gospel so that we can overcome resistance and bless and protect and save others for God. Where would God be without our PR campaign?

But what if the power of God was given to us not so that we could win but so that we would have the spiritual fortitude to *lose*? What if the gospel is the power of God given to us not so that we would have the vigor and shrewdness to seize power but so that we would have the integrity and strength to remain faithful, even in our powerlessness? What if the power of God is made available to us so that we would have the wisdom and grace to follow Jesus into the weakness, loss, failure, and despair that are unavoidable byproducts of living faithfully in a culture of violence, hierarchy, and supremacy?

We're all used to having Paul's words "I can do all things through Christ who strengthens me" shoved down our throats as the unquestionable authority on Christian living (Phil 4:13; NKJV). We are taught that he has the last word of how we are and are not allowed to behave. *Don't question, don't argue, don't talk back; it's this way because Paul said so, fall in line!* But we forget (or are strategically not taught) that during his life, Paul was not a powerful authority figure. Anyone who *was* seen as a powerful authority figure in Paul's world saw him as a foolish, weak loser. A man who once had minor authority and respectability as a Pharisee with a good pedigree, Paul inexplicably threw it away to seek out a marginal living as a tentmaker while preaching the gospel of a dead, fringe cult leader who was disavowed by his own people.

Paul was a nobody, a joke. There is an unholy irony in the way Christian leaders have used Paul's words to justify exerting ruthless authority and control over vulnerable people. Paul of Tarsus wrote from the underside of history, as one who renounced a position of power and authority over others in order to take on an extremely vulnerable, new identity. His letters encouraged small, beleaguered communities as they embodied, at great personal cost and risk, the teachings of Christ in defiance of the dominant power structures.

Most of the letters we have from Paul were written while he was in prison, awaiting execution. His churches were full of weirdos, outcasts, and suckers. When Paul assured the church in Rome that he wasn't ashamed, the average Roman citizen (who wouldn't have known his name or read his letter in the first place) would have said, "Why the hell not?" In an honor-shame culture, Paul's choices to forsake the status and privilege of his identity as a Roman citizen and a wealthy and powerful Pharisee and align himself with poor gentiles made no sense. Two thousand years later, his words have power. But in his lifetime, there was only one word to describe him: loser.

And yet, all these years later, we expect the power of God contained in the gospel to make *us* powerful winners. That's not what it did for Paul, but why should we pay attention to the life of that guy? We insist that following Jesus will make us successful and celebrated and bulletproof. This is an extraordinary expectation, unless you believe that the current expression of culture is a fairly accurate representation of the culture of the kingdom of heaven. Last time I checked, neither side of the culture war believed that. So it's irrational to believe that the power of God will make you a winner as the contemporary world crowns winners.

The power of God is the power to resist. It is the power to lose.

* * *

For most of my life I have tried to be a winner. So when two-thirds of the members of the congregation I was pastoring left, convinced that I'd destroyed their beloved church in a vain pursuit of power and glory, I told myself having a hard first call didn't make me a loser, and I could still turn things around. When a deal to yoke our church with another congregation fell apart at the last minute, and when the remaining members of the congregation concluded that we had no chance of survival, and when we applied and were summarily rejected for denominational loans, I told myself that other people just didn't understand what we were trying to do—yet. But they'd come around. When we applied for civic grants and were rejected, and when I requested the committee comments and saw that they actually mocked us for applying, I told myself they were rude and that they'd come to see and appreciate us someday.

But finally, when the church transformation program we were in was abruptly discontinued by the presbytery, and when the consultants, who were on their way out, warned us that we were certain to fail if we pursued our foolish dream of a multiethnic congregation reflective of our neighborhood context, and when we were hemorrhaging money and roping off empty pews in an attempt to make worship feel less desolate: Then, finally, it became impossible to numb my internal shame and dread of failure. For more than a year, every time I closed my eyes, I could see nothing but the handwriting on the wall. And that handwriting said we were idiots to try to change our ways so that we could share our sacred community with our neighbors. Who would want to be part of a dying church like ours? I could no longer pretend that I didn't feel like a failure.

During this stretch—when we were not growing but not quite dying, a time when we had stopped being the church we were but had not yet figured out how to become the church we would one day be—a wise and generous mentor advised me to do two things. Cut the budget, which meant finding severance for our part-time administrator, halving my own salary, unenrolling myself in denominational healthcare and pension programs, and taking on much of the administrative work myself. When I balked, she gently told me, "What you have now is the budget of a much larger church; you don't need that anymore."

But what came next was exponentially more painful. The second thing I had to do in that liminal in-between season was call every person who was leaving the church and offer them pastoral care. Invite them to coffee or lunch and just listen to everything they had to say without defensiveness or excuses. I wasn't calling to argue or convince; that time was past. I was calling because love listens to people in pain.

After days of doing this work (it's amazing how suddenly large my congregation seemed), I called my mentor in tears. It's excruciating to listen to people you love tell you how much you failed them. It didn't matter that I was doing my best to be faithful; they were wounded. I asked my mentor why it was so important to make these calls.

She replied, "God will not let new people come if the old people are cast away. The way you care for these people will make room for new life." And my defenses were down, and I had no strength for anything but cringeworthy vulnerability. I gave voice to my brokenness and despair, "But new people *won't* come! Why would anyone come to our half-dead, bad-at-everything church? I can't make people come."

And she said, "Of course you can't. All you can do is care well for the people who are there and the people who are leaving. Only the Holy Spirit can lead people to your church, and the Holy Spirit doesn't work for you." She gave me a long moment to absorb the enormity of that truth I had spent years running from. "Your job is to be faithful and trust God. You don't get to control the results." Then she encouraged me to pray.

I hung up, wondering if I still wanted to call and listen to the people who hated me. Would I still choose to pastor the leaving ones in this painful way if it wasn't some sort of magical guarantee I'd get to serve a growing church? Freed of a quid pro quo masquerading as faith, I had a pure decision to make: Did I believe in loving and caring for people or not? Without knowing what Jesus would do for me, would I still choose to serve people for Jesus?

* * *

It was only when I faced inevitable loss that I was ready to think about the power of gospel being the power to lose.

The wise saints in the church who stayed in the sinking ship with me were far ahead of me. I was only becoming ready to listen. They already understood. In that season of perpetual loss, a local nonprofit leader offered to mediate some sessions with departed church members; she counseled seeking reconciliation with those who had left in the hope that they (and their financial support) might return, restore our broken body, and allow the church to survive a little longer. Full of guilt and shame, I took the proposal to our leadership board. They promptly and resoundingly rejected it. They told me that anyone was welcome to return, and anyone was welcome to join us in our mission to serve our neighbors in humility and love. They agreed that we were surely going to lose the battle to revitalize the congregation. We were going to die.

Having accepted this, they told me our only choice was *how* we would die. There was power in our loss. If we couldn't get out of it, we could seek to be faithful in it. We could choose the story our death would tell. Would people say of us, "That church was a community of people who held on to what they had for as long as they could"? Or would they say, "That church of foolish old white people died trying to become a multiethnic, multigenerational congregation serving its neighbors"? In their brave no, the wise leaders in our church taught me that it was more faithful to lose, even to die, trying to become a church that reflected the culture of the kingdom of God than to "win" by surviving as long as possible.

We're so certain that the power of God is given to make us winners, but what if we're wrong? What if we have the power of God so that we can follow Jesus in the way of losing? What if we are given the power to lose so that we will speak truth to power even when it will cost us everything? What if the power of the gospel is given to us so that we can endure being maligned and misunderstood? What if the power of God is given to us so that Jesus can be our way and not our mascot? So that we can reject the false gospel that "Jesus suffered so we don't have to"? What if the power of God is available to us, not so that we can win, but so that we can see the glory of holding nothing back in the pursuit of righteousness, surrendering not only our institutions but even our lives? What if we need the power of God to lose? In dominant American culture, a God who empowers us to lose is well-hidden indeed.

Our church leadership team decided that day that we could stand to look like fools and losers if it meant bearing witness not to what the world thought a church should be but what the body of Christ already was. We decided to show up every day, for as long as we could, and make the next right faithful choice.

I think of Paul in his prison cell, waiting every day to be executed, knowing he'd never be free again. Whatever influence and impact he'd had as a church planter on the edges of nowhere, those days were behind him. I think of him, still waking up every morning, sitting there writing letters to his tiny little churches. Agonizing over each word, even though he knew there was a great chance they would never reach their audience. And even if they got there, what were the chances they'd be seen as wisdom? Who wants spiritual teaching from a prisoner on death row?

Yet by the power of God, he wasn't ashamed of the gospel that landed him in that prison cell, that made him a joke even among fellow Christians. He kept waking up and choosing the tiny ways of faithfulness that were available to him, trusting they would matter somehow, someway. I believe this is the power of God. It is not the power to force others to do anything. It is Christ's steadfast faithfulness within us, that is not of us, to endure to what seems like the end.

* * *

When I think about how God hides in losing, I think about another man named Paul. Paul Farmer was not a practicing Christian as far as I know. But when I look at his life, I see the power of God revealed in a life unafraid of failure. I believe we can learn more about the right use of the power of God from Paul Farmer's books, *To Repair the World* or *In the Company of the Poor*, than from most Christian bestsellers.

Farmer had an MD and a PhD, and he was a Harvard professor, a clinician, and a social entrepreneur. He was brilliant, but there is a lot of brilliance in this world. His stunning contribution was not his genius but his willingness to lose. As a highly privileged and accomplished white man, Farmer could have won the jobs with the highest salary and greatest prestige. But he told the truth about the winners of this world from Haiti, where he chose to live and do the majority of his work. He didn't imagine a new world so much as he told the damn truth about this one.

As a student, he was taught that it was impossible to treat drug-resistant tuberculosis (TB) in the so-called developing world. He called that out as a lie. He named the feigned ignorance and pretend incapability in the room. Powerful Western leaders perpetuated the myth that the people of Haiti suffered because they were ignorant and incapable of maintaining health care systems. Farmer declared it was North Americans, pretending to be ignorant and impotent, who perpetuated the systems delivering inequitable global outcomes. When he got to the tables where policy decisions were being made, he showed up not to win power or prestige but to tell the truth—even if it got him banned for life. Of course we can treat drug-resistant TB in Haiti. We treat it in the United States. We treat it in Canada. We treat it in Europe. We have the drugs, and we have the medical technology. We can treat drug-resistant TB anywhere in any body. It is not the rarified air of a particular country that makes the drugs efficacious; it's the resources and policies that grant access to treatment. When policymakers say a treatable disease can't be treated, what they mean is powerful people in nongovernmental organizations and the philanthropy world have come together and agreed that they *won't* treat bodies with drug-resistant TB in certain geographical regions. It's a collective collusion of pretend incapability that renders everyone innocent.

Farmer refused to perpetuate the lie, and his demands for equity made everyone uncomfortable. Stakeholders argued back that it was a question of resources. Sure, biologically speaking, diseased bodies in the developing world could be treated. But economically, it couldn't be done. In response, Farmer started quoting statistics about Halloween costumes and pets. He pointed out that not only are Halloween costumes a multibillion-dollar industry, so are Halloween costumes for dogs. He refused to sit at tables where powerful people pretended there wasn't enough money to treat curable diseases in some parts of the planet when there was enough money in the world to buy Halloween costumes for dogs. "You shall know the truth, and the truth shall make you free," Jesus said (John 8:32; NKJV). Some of us Christians preach that. Farmer lived it. He told the truth, even though it offended and angered powerful people. He told the truth about the way health care worked and argued for a better way, even though it lost him friends and influence and opportunities. Farmer was born with privileges and advantages, and he leveraged them to get to the places where decisions were being made. Once he got there, he didn't try to win awards and accolades. He told the truth about our complicity in one another's suffering.

Farmer understood that glory often lies in defeat. He warned of the danger of wanting to save the world: "We want to be on the winning team, but at the risk of turning our backs on the losers, no, it's not worth it. So we fight the long defeat." He advocated for losing, for leveraging all the power and ability one has to embrace the long defeat. Farmer's philosophy of public health was searingly simple: The well should help the sick. Not only the conveniently located sick, not only the sick who are likely to recover, not only the sick whose recovery will be visible and permanent, and not only the sick who can afford premium health insurance plans. The well should help all the sick, especially those who will not recover, those who are likely to die or relapse, and those who won't have a "successful" outcome.

The well should help the sick: It echoes the health care philosophy of Jesus, who said "it is not the healthy who need a doctor, but the sick" (Matt 9:12). If this is your health care philosophy, you are going to lose a lot of patients because you will be investing time and resources on dying people whom others would pass by. Your stats will make you look less skilled than a practitioner who is more discriminating in selecting patients. But because of your willingness to risk defeat, vulnerable people will have a chance to be healed.

Jesus's life shows us that there is glory and honor and power in choosing the long defeat. Like the pearl of great price or the treasure buried in a field, you will find God hidden in failure. But it will cost you everything.

* * *

When I think about what it looks like to manifest the power of God to lose, I also think of Corrie ten Boom. I discovered her story when I plucked a book off the shelf of a dusty church library shelf, intrigued by the title: *Tramp for the Lord*. I had no idea what was inside, but I was pretty sure I was going to make fun of it.

Instead, I found the story of a Dutch Christian family who were empowered by the gospel to resist the Nazi regime. They risked their own safety to hide Jewish strangers in their home. And their righteousness did not protect them. The ten Boom family was betrayed and imprisoned in concentration camps along with those they sought to protect. Corrie ten Boom survived, but she lost everyone she loved, everyone who had taught her how to follow Christ, to the powers of violence and death and nationalism. And then she devoted her postwar life to preaching the gospel to a defeated and guilty German nation.

Astonishingly, one day after she had preached about forgiveness, the very guard who had been most cruel to her in a concentration camp came to her and asked her to forgive him. He stood there before her, holding out his hand.

The power of God did not protect her family, and neither did it shield her from the pain and anguish of grieving their deaths. But after an internal struggle, ten Boom was able to call upon the power of God to give her the ability to shake his hand. This led to embracing him, weeping with him, and reconciling with him. As she recounts the story in her memoir, she had no natural desire to forgive the guard. She prayed that God would give her both the physical strength to lift her hand and the spiritual desire to be reconciled with him. In that moment, in answer to that prayer, in body and soul, she became a conduit of the power of God. She shook his hand and began to authentically rejoice in his forgiveness. This is not an easy power to celebrate. The power to forgive the unforgivable is not a power we desire.

The Christian industrial complex sanctimoniously declares that lives full of the power of God will be known by their successful resumes, their security, and their satisfaction. Many preachers seek to entice people to Jesus by preaching that if you do right, the power of God will ensure that life will go right for you. Conversely, this means that loss, failure, and suffering are proof that you are sinful and far from God. The power of God must be against you because God backs winners. Pain becomes an indicator of moral failing, and avoiding pain becomes synonymous with righteousness. Losers need not apply for membership in the body of Christ. The church in America has cosigned on this myth. That's why we love the story of someone who has overcome systemic injustice and oppression. Those stories allow us to pretend that the systems aren't toxic, that the power of God is sufficient for anyone who really matters. The American empire self-referentially declares that people get what they deserve here. Maybe not immediately but eventually, always.

The kingdom of Jesus makes no similar promises to us about life this side of eternity. The gospel of Jesus Christ reveals real righteousness and then gives us the grace and power to embody it, albeit imperfectly. There are promises of light burdens, easy yokes, provision, and abundant life. But there are no empire promises that if we do well, all will always go well for us. In fact, the Bible says the opposite. "I am sending you out like sheep among wolves," Jesus says (Matt 10:16) "I will not allow your foot to slip," God says (Ps 121:3; my translation). But sometimes he will allow your whole, holy self to be crushed. We are not given the power of God so that we will embrace winning. Who needs spiritual strength to bear the burden of too much winning? No, the gospel of Jesus Christ is given to empower us to bear the stigma and pain of failure and loss, because that will inevitably be part of our journey.

* * *

When I think about the high cost of true discipleship, a cost that many who follow Christ are unwilling to pay because they believe he guarantees them safe and pleasurable victory, I also think of the Charleston Nine, gathered in their sanctuary on a humid Wednesday night in June 2015. They welcomed in a stranger, opened the Scriptures with him, prayed with him. And then he rose from his chair, took out a gun, and began to shoot them.

They welcomed him in, this young white man. He fit the description of the American terrorists who had been lynching and persecuting their ancestors for generations, but by the power of the gospel, they received him in as a lost brother. Then he murdered them. He murdered Rev. Clementa Pinckney. He murdered Cynthia Hurd. He murdered Rev. Sharonda Coleman-Singleton. He murdered Tywanza Sanders. He murdered Ethel Lance. He murdered Susie Jackson. He murdered Depayne Middleton-Doctor. He murdered Rev. Daniel Simmons. He murdered Myra Thompson. I think about Rev. Pinckney's wife and children who were waiting for him in his office down the hall and heard it all.

And then the murderer fled. He was later arrested and safely escorted into custody. While he was being processed, and before the bodies of the dead had even been removed from the blood-soaked sanctuary, officers brought him food from a nearby Burger King.

I think about the holy cherished ones who were martyred that night. They were the kind of people who make their way back to the church to study Scripture together in the middle of the week. Two of them were the kind of retired pastors who still gathered to pray in the sanctuary with the flock, because gathering in community around the word of God wasn't what they did for a living but who they were. I think about how they were killed because of their deep commitment to the way of Jesus. Had they gathered in safety and security, in a private and locked location, had they turned away the stranger, had they been carrying weapons of their own, they would have been safe. Instead, they choose to live like all those sent by Christ, as "sheep among wolves" (Matt 10:16). The world is not worthy of their witness.

I think about their grieving loved ones, who came to bear witness to the power of God at the arraignment just a few days later. One by one, they stood up before the watching world and looked into the face of the one who killed their loved ones. And they testified to the brutality, to the horror, to the evilness of the lies that possessed him. They counted the cost, the incalculably precious bodies shattered by bullets, their own hearts that will never beat again without pain, the wounds they carry. And then, by the power of God, some offered forgiveness to the one who murdered their beloved ones. Those who forgave didn't do so because the murderer wasn't responsible for his actions. They forgave him because he was. They forgave him to bear witness to an even greater power than his violence and hate. In forgiving him they embodied the transcendent and triumphant power of holy love. This is the way of Christ that we cannot fathom. It is hard to speak of such holiness. To put it into words risks profaning it. Yet how can we not bear witness to their testimony?

The wisdom of this age seeks to win against evil by destroying threats and evildoers. But the power of God is a love that does not protect itself but pours itself out for the salvation of others. Their words are an echo of the words Jesus cried out from the cross, "Father, forgive them, for they do not know what they do" (Luke 23:34; NKJV). This is the power of God. It is not the power to destroy or avenge but the power to choose to not seek vengeance. It is the ability to seek blessing for one's bitterest enemies, not because they aren't really your enemies but because they really, truly are. It is not celebrated by the watching world because to the world it does not look like victory. But it is the triumph of souls who, like Christ, have overcome the world. This is the power of resurrection life that neither condones, ignores, nor yields to evil, but defiantly insists that only love will endure.

* * *

In my ongoing struggle to seek God in my own life, I try to set aside time to be still. In the mornings I try to pray Psalm 27:3–5, which says:

Though an army besiege me,
my heart will not fear;
though war break out against me,
even then will I be confident.
One thing I ask of the Lord,
this only do I seek:
that I may dwell in the house of the Lord
all the days of my life,
to gaze upon the beauty of the Lord
and to seek him in his temple.
For in the day of trouble
he will keep me safe in his dwelling.

This is a prayer of cruciform hope. The desire to be with God no matter what is a desire shaped by the revelation of the cross. The prayer longs not for wealth, winning, or false peace, but the beautiful life that is found in the presence of the Lord, even when the day of trouble comes.

Sometimes a false gospel lands like a lantern fly, its wings patterned with beautiful illusions that days of trouble will never come for those who love and are loved by God. This invasive, destructive, false gospel breeds death. It is not lost on me that when I went to write about those who triumphed through failure and loss, the stories that came to me were that of a white man who served in Haiti, a white woman who survived the Holocaust, and Black Christians made martyrs, not by choice but through the inexorable appetite of white supremacy. I want to share stories of white American Christians who have kept the faith, undeterred by the high cost and real risks of picking up Christ's cross and bearing witness to a love more powerful than violence and death, a love more valuable than wealth and worldly power. But those witnesses are hard to find among white American Christians when our collective sense of what following Jesus entails has been more shaped by the shallow lies of the false gospel than the deep truths of the life, death, and resurrection of Jesus Christ.

The real gospel, foolish stumbling block that it is, promises to strengthen and bear us up even when the opposition is near and very much against you. The real gospel, which is hidden from those who seek to succeed in the world as it is, says that sometimes following Jesus must lead to rejection, arrest, abandonment, and even death. The good news the gospel announces is that you can dwell deeply in the presence of God even and especially in times of suffering and loss. The real gospel says that, even for beloved and faithful ones, sometimes the cancer scan reveals the worst possible scenario; sometimes the one you love most stops loving you back; sometimes there isn't a last-minute reprieve, and the sheriff comes to change the locks; sometimes you are the one who is laid off, and you don't know how you will afford your insulin; sometimes welcoming in the stranger and loving your enemies is a death sentence; sometimes the worst things happen to you, and that isn't a sign that God has turned against you. Strangely, even infuriatingly, injustice and tragedy can become the source of new, richer life with Christ. As Corrie ten Boom testified again and again in her speeches and writings, you can only learn that Jesus is sufficient when Jesus is all that you have.

Let's not pretend that we are any better than Peter and the rest of the disciples who desperately sought to turn Jesus back from the cross. We do not choose the road of suffering or loss, nor does the Lord require us to. But when the path of faithfulness leads through the valley of despair, the power of God is available to us. Too often we compromise with evil because we refuse to believe that God would ask us to sacrifice, to suffer, or to risk our health or our safety or our status. So we assert our right to bear arms, because we have to protect ourselves. We vote against the best interests of our neighbors, because we have to look out for number one. We stay home from the protests because we might get hurt, and they won't make any difference anyway. We smile politely at the racist joke because we don't want to appear self-righteous or "woke" or make anyone uncomfortable.

The world doesn't need people who are willing to win at all costs for Jesus. The gospel doesn't entitle us to the shallow best the culture has to offer. The gospel reveals to us the beauty of God's kingdom, a realm of shalom and kinship and community borne out of trinity, where hierarchies and threats are forged into beloved communities of blessing.

The world needs people so captivated by this vision of life with Jesus that they are willing to lose anything and risk everything in order to bear witness to this salvation way. The church needs people so in tune with the wild beauty of Christ's song that they won't stop singing it, even though it gets them labeled naive fools and failures. The church needs people too committed to loving and healing the world to wait to start until it loves and respects them back. The church needs disciples who look at the cross and understand that it is the ultimate victory—of love over fear, peace over violence, forgiveness over hate, life over death. The church needs holy losers. A lot of them. They are the ones who can show us the way into free and abundant life.

Part III

SMALL

Seeing the Glory of Infinitesimal Things

9

NOTHING GOOD COULD HAPPEN HERE

ANYONE WHO HAS ever shopped for anything in December in the Northern Hemisphere knows that Jesus was born in Bethlehem, whether they want to or not. The juggernaut of the Christian industrial complex ensures that everyone knows the little town of Bethlehem is where the little Lord Jesus lay in a manger, his holiness ensuring that no crying he makes. Ubiquity and familiarity mean no one finds the fact that Jesus was born in Bethlehem interesting or surprising. This is a shame, because it is both. If Jesus is the Messiah, the Son of God and Savior of the world, he *should* have been born in Jerusalem.

King David established Jerusalem as the capital of the nation of Israel, the holy city of the promised land. In psalms and prophecy, Jerusalem is revered as the mount of God, the house of the Lord, the footstool of the heavenly throne room, and the umbilical cord connecting heaven and earth. For centuries, the devout made sacred pilgrimage to Jerusalem to worship in the Temple, singing the songs of ascent on their way. Where else could the cosmic Redeemer of creation be born but in "the house of the Lord" on the mount of Zion which "cannot be shaken but endures forever" (Ps 125)? Surely, the sacred, noncrying baby should have been laying in the "resting place" and "dwelling place" of the God of Jacob, the place from which God "bestows his blessing, even life forevermore" (Ps 133). The name Jerusalem comes from the Hebrew words *yi'reh*, meaning "he will see to it," and *sha'lem*, a derivation of shalom, meaning "peace." So, etymologically, the city is "the place from which God will bring peace." Of course the Prince of Peace would be born there.

The name Bethlehem, in contrast, means "house of bread." It sounds like the place you go to run errands or grab a sandwich, not seek a savior. Which is why, famously, the wise men didn't seek the King of the Jews in Bethlehem. They followed the star, but once they got close to Jerusalem, they switched off satnav and went to the palace. Because of course that's where any newborn King of the Jews would be.

Except he wasn't. He was in Bethlehem, as foretold by the prophet Micah: "But you, Bethlehem Ephrathah, though you are small among the clans of Judah, out of you will come for me one who will be ruler over Israel" (Mic 5:2). Ironically, Micah's prophecy was fulfilled through imperial fiat: "In those days Caesar Augustus issued a decree that a census should be taken of the entire Roman world . . . and everyone went to their own town to register" (Luke 2:1, 3). And so, Jesus was born in the ancestral city of Joseph: Bethlehem. This small, insignificant hill city would soon pay for that honor with the blood of other mothers' sons. When King Herod discovered that the wise men had returned to their native lands without revealing to him the exact location of his newborn rival, he ordered the execution of every male child under the age of two. Joseph, forewarned in a dream, took his family and escaped to Egypt, and the hills surrounding Bethlehem echoed with the inconsolable grief of the mothers whose babies were not spared. The King of kings, Lord of lords, and Prince of Peace entered into history on the margins, six miles south of Jerusalem. You might be thinking that six miles is pretty close. But the point isn't that Bethlehem was so far away. The point is that it was a marginal place, known for being on the edge of somewhere else. It's the "almost famous" of cities.

After a stint as a refugee in Egypt, Jesus moved from the edge of nowhere to the middle of it, growing up in Nazareth, in rural Galilee. Nazareth had a reputation for not mattering, prompting one of Jesus's first disciples, Nathanael, to ask frankly and famously if anything good could come from there—to which Jesus replied (and I paraphrase), "He's not lying." John swaps the nativity story for a nativity poem, but it also highlights the irony of Jesus's incarnation, noting that "though the world was made through him, the world did not recognize him" and "he came to that which was his own but his own did not receive him" (John 1:10–11).

There are many reasons Jesus remained an incognito Messiah, even as he calmed storms, walked on water, multiplied loaves and fishes, cast out demons, taught with authority, healed the deaf, blind, and leprous, raised the dead, and walked around with Moses and Elijah on a mountaintop like a human glow stick. Strangely, Jesus himself did his best to turn down the hype, always telling people and demons to keep his identity to themselves. But many people couldn't see who he was because of where he was from. It wasn't just what he said but the accent he said it with. Once they heard where he was from, they believed they knew who he could be. Born in Bethlehem, raised in Nazareth, hanging out in Galilee: These were all small, rural, insignificant places, the kind we ironically still insist on calling "godforsaken." Of course the long-awaited messiah couldn't have grown up in *Nazareth*. Nobody who matters is born in *Bethlehem*. For that matter, nobody of earthly or heavenly importance would have had to run for their lives to Egypt as a refugee.

We still miss God's presence in the places we refuse to look for it. We still believe our expectations are God's limits. Formed by a culture that celebrates corporate mergers, economies of scale, and health care consolidation, we do not know how to imagine a greatness that isn't large and universal. We are confident the next great political leader won't come out of a flyover state. We are sure there aren't any biblical interpreters worth reading who didn't go to seminary. We assume everything becomes more valuable the larger it grows: bank accounts, muscles, diamond rings, earnings reports, or book sales. The cream—the best and richest part—always rises to the top, right? And the top is Jerusalem, the top is the Ivy League, the top is the upper-middle-class whose churches have endowments and political influence and pipe organs. We expect good things to flow from the center out. We believe holy things trickle down from the top.

But Jesus disrupts that simple toxic narrative. The Son of God was born at the bottom, chose to live on the margins, and insisted on hanging around with nobodies. To the casual observer, Jesus looked like someone who had potential but didn't realize it, someone who could have been somebody but decided not to be. Jesus came from small and never scaled up. He never got past where he came from. And those of us whose faith was formed by the Christian industrial complex see the small scale of Jesus's life as embarrassing instead as revelatory.

* * *

A kind older pastor was horrified when he learned that I was accepting a call to serve as the temporary pastor of the church where I still serve. He pulled me aside and encouraged me to wait for something bigger, in a better part of town. My mentor explained to me that the previous pastor had tried everything and that if that church could be saved, it would have been already. He told me I was a promising pastor and that I should wait for a promising call.

I knew young women didn't get called to lead churches unless they were small and in steep decline, so I went anyway. It was inconceivable to either of us that the church didn't need saving from its size or marginality. Both of us assumed that the size of the congregation and the reputation of the neighborhood were liabilities, not assets.

I arrived at my new church in early December. A few weeks later, as if to prove that pastor's point, the local paper featured a story about our neighborhood entitled "A Cluster of Desperation." As familiar as I was with the geographical details of Jesus's life, as eager as I was to preach my first Christmas sermons, it never occurred to me that I had anything to learn from them in my new ministry. The details of the story were facts, not revelations. I had hope because Jesus was born but not because of where he was born and grew up, not because of where he chose to practice his ministry. The geography of Christ's life didn't have any special significance for me then. But now, for me, that map has become a lifeline.

Jesus was born into small and placed by God on the margins. When he could have gone elsewhere, he didn't. In an imperial world where bigger was always better, might made right, and more was more, Jesus sanctified small. And when he talked about his kingdom, he centered small. His beatitudes sanctified the meek and the weak, the poor and powerless. He celebrated the extraordinary generosity and power of the widow's mite. He wasn't blinded by size. He told us that the kingdom would swell forth from small things: a tiny mustard seed, one obedient son, one found coin, a single grain of wheat fallen to the ground. The things we cower before—the rulers and authorities, the grandeur of the Temple, the powers and principalities, the kings and empires—will all pass away. Visible though they are, their power is an illusion.

It's clear to me now that Jesus is trying to redeem our spiritual imaginations, as impoverished as they are by the dominant narrative of an imperial culture. He's showing us that God's power is not channeled through our fallen institutions. God's power is not limited by our powerlessness, but flourishes within it.

So David doesn't have to be big enough to fit into Saul's armor or strong enough to lift up his sword. By the power of God, a slingshot brings down a giant. In other stories, a shout demolishes a city wall, a stick separates the sea, a donkey's jawbone defeats a battalion, and the sound made by one-third of a small army breaking jars turns three invading armies against one another and delivers the victory. It's what Paul meant when he said, "If God is for us, who can be against us?" (Rom 8:31). The apostle isn't saying "God is on our side, so we can do whatever terrible thing we want." He's saying we no longer have to fear the repercussions of practicing Christ's radical way of mercy, enemy love, and subversive gentleness. God's power is not only more beautiful, but it is also greater than the powers of this world. But if fear compels us to conform to imperial power, then God's power is against us.

The church I serve hosts a free community meal on the second Tuesday of every month. The tagline is "come when you can, leave when you're ready." There is no program, no agenda, no purpose other than to break bread with neighbors and friends and strangers. The volunteers who prepare the food and set the tables believe there is no higher or holier purpose than that. I love those nights. I am chief of the clean-up crew, a prolific chair stacker and table breaker-downer. And not to brag, but I've done it all in heels with a baby strapped to my back.

Mostly, though, my role is to walk around and talk to everybody, because I am the pastor. This is often difficult for people to understand, partly because our building doesn't have a steeple and they came for a community meal and didn't realize it was happening in a church. But also, because I am told I do not—ahem—*look* like a pastor. A lot of people are surprised, but some people are downright offended. They'll tell me, "I'm sorry, but I don't believe in women pastors." To which I smile and say, "Well, I believe in you, and it's nice to meet you."

Frequently people ask me, not unkindly, how I can expect to have authority over the men in my congregation. I start by gently explaining to them that it's not my congregation; it belongs to Jesus. Then I tell them that I don't expect to have authority over anyone, not because I am a woman, but because I am a disciple of Jesus Christ. "Jesus is the sole authority around here, and the rest of us are friends who serve him together." Once, a couple pulled me aside and told me they had a ministry and they believed that God was leading them to operate it out of our building—but they'd have to talk to my husband first. To which I thought, "Well, you'll have to catch him first." Literally. My husband is an introvert who runs five mornings a week and can still finish a 5K race in less than twenty minutes.

Growing up Catholic, he certainly never anticipated becoming a pastor's spouse. He is open to relationships with people in the church and serves as he feels called, but he's baffled by the expectation that he be involved in ministry because he's my husband. Early in our marriage he stopped me as I was trying to convince him to help me out with an understaffed initiative. He said, "That's your job, not mine. I don't ask you to do part of my work. Please don't ask me to do part of yours." So I'd pay good money to watch someone ask my husband if I had his permission to launch a new ministry initiative.

I choose to be amused by these memories now, but I wasn't at the time. They were humiliating, but they also worried me. I feared my gender was a real liability to the church, because so many of the people I was meeting, who might be wonderful members of the community, turned around and walked away once they learned I was the pastor. They were open to collaborating with my husband, who they'd never met and who wasn't called to pastoral ministry, but not with me. We had so many factors working against us already; what if my gender was the straw that broke the camel's back? I wondered if it was selfish for me to stay on as a pastor if it meant a large portion of the not-very-large portion of people seeking a congregation would never consider ours.

I do believe my gender is one of the factors that shapes our community. It is undeniably a stumbling block for many people seeking a church. But now I think that stumbling block is a great gift. Those who are searching for a traditional, large, hierarchical congregation will walk past ours, and that's okay. Those who believe the church should be led by one man with ultimate authority over them will look elsewhere. I don't think we're better off without those people, but I do think we're healthier without that patriarchal expectation. I do think we're better off because we can't access that kind of power. Hierarchical structures with chains of command are more efficient, but I am beginning to think efficiency is a limiting factor in spiritual formation. When you can only grow at the rate you can cultivate deep, healthy, spiritual friendships, you don't grow big or fast, but you do grow sustainably.

When you spend more than a decade pastoring a marginal church that once only had three months to live, you begin to understand that it is God who sustains. And the way God sustains is through small. Small gifts, small beginnings, small steps, small wins, small voices. In the world outside our doors, these are unseen and uncounted because they are deemed unimportant. But when you live in the struggle, it is small things that keep you.

There are many people who no longer believe that the large, centered, and celebrated institutions can keep their promises. There are lots of folks who know in their flesh that the old ways deliver nothing but illusions and death. And when the grace of God is manifested through those people and their beautifully imperfect little gifts, there is more than enough for abundance.

While I was still in seminary, I taught a children's Sunday school class in a basement. Some days we had twelve children. Some days we had four. And I knew that what happened in that room was more important than any grade I earned in graduate school. Most of the children lived around the corner and walked to the church by themselves. Many of their families had immigrated to the city from other parts of the world. I marveled at the steadfast, selfless love of their parents, often leaving behind their own hard-won professional identities as bankers and physicians and teachers and working the essential low-wage jobs that our culture dishonors to launch their children into a world that, in many ways, they themselves would never inhabit.

We learned Scripture together down there in the church basement, the children and me. I was sharing stories I barely knew, and we puzzled them out together. We prayed and sang songs and made art and hung our pictures on the wall and learned to ask one another the most important question: "What do you think God is showing us in this story?"

At the end of one year, we sat in a circle on the floor, sharing cupcakes and juice, and I asked them to teach us what was most important to them in our faith. We went around the circle and they opened their hearts. I treasured their answers. Young voices finding courage in Ruth's refusing to leave Naomi, inspiration in Joshua making the sun stand still, hope and dignity in the humble details of Jesus's birth.

One child's answer I remember almost daily. George was twelve, so he'd almost aged out of our class. He was born in Vietnam. He was tall and thin with serious brown eyes. He came infrequently. His peers were boisterous, but George was quiet. When he did speak, we all listened. That day he told us his most important story was the time Jesus told Peter to catch the one fish.

Initially, I thought he was conflating several stories. It took me a while to figure out he was remembering the time some tax collectors came to Peter asking, "Doesn't your teacher pay the temple tax?" (Matt 17:24). Peter indignantly insisted that Jesus did and walked away. Jesus, who wasn't there, followed up with Peter in a complex philosophical teaching about his identity as the Son of God. He reminded Peter that in earthly kingdoms it is the subjects, not the heirs of kings, who pay taxes, so he, as the Son of God, was exempt from the tax on his own Father's house. But Jesus directed Peter to pay the tax anyway, instructing him to take his fishing line and cast it into the lake. "Take the first fish you catch; open its mouth and you will find a four-drachma coin. Take it and give it to them for my tax and yours" (Matt 17:27).

I thought it was odd that a twelve-year-old boy was interested in a story about Jesus's hidden messianic identity, Temple maintenance, and the theology of taxation. I asked him to help me understand why this story was so important to him. It seemed to me to have so little to do with his lived experience. George said it was because of the fish. He said he liked to think about how Jesus knew exactly what was inside of that particular fish. It looked the same as every other fish in the lake. But inside, there was something good—something small and essential—that only Jesus could see.

At church and in seminary, I was taught to read that story from the top down. My heart was drawn to what was powerful and large—the grandeur of the Temple, the majesty of Jesus as the Son of God Almighty, the conflict between authority of powerful sacred institutions and spiritual authority of Christ. I studied that text to learn how to negotiate the "world that is," to learn what obligations I had the holy authority to defy.

George read the story from the bottom up. He didn't care about the Temple or taxes or the dangers of civil religion. George and his family struggled to navigate the crushing bureaucracy of the American immigration system; his parents worked several full-time, minimum-wage jobs just to survive at the bottom of a ruthless economy that labeled them "unskilled." George knew there were some forces that could not be placated or denied. He knew this wasn't a matter of philosophy but survival.

His heart was fixed on the fish and the coin—the smallest, most humble elements of the story—and how the glory of God perceived the worthiness and power they carry within. Many people in his community saw George as just one more immigrant child draining the system, interchangeable with any other. But the spirit of God instilled within George the knowledge of his own inviolable, sacred worth through this story, which wasn't really about taxation or institutions or power struggles at all.

For all the years I've studied this text, all the scholarly treatises I've read upon it, I've never come across anyone else who saw what George saw in that text. As I continue to seek the wisdom and strength to give my life to a small and precious community whose value is invisible to the culture surrounding it, George's insight nourishes me. There is what a thing appears to be, and there is what it is. The two are not the same.

I marveled at the lesson George taught me. I remembered it, but I didn't want to live it. I know small isn't bad. I know size is no indicator of sacred worth. Here I am, writing a book about the theological value of small. And still, it feels like a gut punch any time anyone describes the congregation I serve as "small." My ego has yet to catch up to my heart.

For George, all the glory lay under the surface of the waters, in the mouth of one fish. Swimming in a lake teeming with other identical fish, that fish was a small thing carrying another small thing, something valuable and necessary.

* * *

Years ago, when we were still in the holy hell of church transformation, I found myself at a luncheon sponsored by executives in my denomination. We were gathered to talk about the future of the national church, and a high-ranking official was giving a presentation about institutional health. He stood in front of us in a suit and tie and warned us that he was going to start with the bad news. He threw up a slide of a bar graph showing that 90 percent of the congregations in our denomination were in steep decline. According to his calculations, none of them would exist in fifteen years. Even more alarmingly to the pastors in the room, he figured most of those churches wouldn't have the financial resources to support a full-time pastor with benefits in five years.

"I told you I was going to start with the bad news," he said, and held up a hand. "But don't panic." And then, I swear, he winked at us. "Because now I'm going to show you the good news, and the good news is so good it makes the bad news not matter." Spoiler alert—the good news wasn't Jesus.

The good news was another slide with a different bar chart. This chart showed the assets of the 10 percent of congregations that were not in decline. He invited us to marvel at the size of their real estate portfolios, their budgets, and, lastly, their congregations. This was really good news because, he explained to us, while it looked bad that 90 percent of the congregations were in decline, 90 percent of the people in our denomination were members in the 10 percent churches. So that meant that the imminent death of congregations didn't matter—because people weren't in those churches anyway. In fact, when those churches closed, their assets would flow to the 10 percent of the churches that were healthy and growing. So "lift up your heads, ye mighty gates"! The death of your brother's church doesn't matter! Everyone who does matters is part of the 10 percent, and the death of the small, weak churches will ensure the everlasting vitality of the large ones!

Then and now, *small* is a dirty word. Small is no longer a description; it's an indictment.

The cognitive dissonance in moments like these is excruciating. I expect the secular world to look at a church like ours commercially and to value it as exponentially less worthy than the land it is built on. I expect developers to believe that the neighborhood would be vastly improved if the church building was torn down and replaced by a Walmart or, better yet, luxury apartments. I expect a hypercapitalist culture to be unable to calculate the sacred worth of a small thing. But when the national leaders of the church also see our community as worth less than the sum total of physical assets? It craters my heart.

On Sundays we preach sermons about one Samaritan turning aside to care for one wounded stranger, of the surpassing worth of a widow's two mites, of five loaves and two fishes becoming feast for a multitude. In our sanctuaries, we tell stories about how in the kingdom there is an inverse correlation between size and power. But in our denominational business meetings, we scorn small, despise weak, and fetishize big and rich.

What do you do when the ones who taught you the faith song, the ones who believe they own the copyright, are no longer interested in living it? What do you do with a church that is interested in serving and saving the small but not becoming one with them?

Small might have become shameful in our eyes. But I know it is not and never has been to Jesus. Not to the One who set aside the glory and power of divinity and made himself small. He set aside all his holy supremacy and fit infinity into the infinitesimal finite—becoming small. Small enough to fit within the swell of a young girl's belly, he traded the waters of cosmic creation for the waters of the womb. If a thousand years are like a day in the Lord's sight, then surely God's sense of the size of a thing is equally inscrutable.

For us, measurements determine magnitude. We are sure that the abundant life in Jesus is expressed in scaling up: more people, more power, more money, more success. And yet we also say that in his incarnation Jesus accomplished the full redemption of all creation. We claim to believe salvation was accomplished through the life of Jesus and that life was small. He was born small, lived small, and chose to stay on the margins, serving the poor and powerless. Then he died, suffering and weak. He could have been anything; he chose to be small.

If the sovereignty of God means anything, it means God designed the incarnation. Jesus could have chosen to be born into power and privilege. He could have courted the wealthy and elite. He could have usurped Caesar's throne and forced a Pax Hebraica. He could have lived high and large. Instead, he went low and tiny. He sanctified the edges.

We Christians say we follow him. We call ourselves disciples, which means learners, and yet we won't let him teach us the sacredness of small. We persist in ignoring who he was as we worship who we wish he'd been, which is really who we hope we'll be. Make us anything, God, just don't make us small.

We have a tradition in the church I serve: Each January, the pastor prays and discerns a word of the year for the congregation. This practice, and the expectation that I will discern the word, unsettles me. I worry that I confuse my own voice with the Lord's, that I will allow my desires and insecurities to mimic the voice of the Lord. I'm worried I'll hear what I want to hear, instead of whatever the Lord has for us.

At least I *used* to worry a lot about that. But then came the year that I sought the Lord for our word and heard *small*. And I knew that didn't come from me because it so deeply challenged and disturbed me that I could barely talk about it. Yes, we were small, but I felt I had to apologize for it. I desperately hoped we'd grow out of it. In that season, the Lord showed me we had to grow *into* it.

Slowly I began to unlearn and understand. If we are aspiring to please and impress the culture, then we must be big and important and impressive. But if we are learning to be who we say we already are, followers of Jesus, then we will let Jesus's life teach us that we do not have to be large to be faithful. We will expect that the inbreaking of the kingdom will be perceived in our day as marginal and foolish, just as it was in the first century. We will not be offended that the culture around us does not already understand the way that is our sacred obligation to embody and teach. A church that's fully conformed to the culture cannot be used by God to transform it.

God is not limited by small. God is not offended by small. We are. The geography of the birth and life of Jesus is not a meaningless data point or a disguise. It's a revelation. Jesus was born on the edges to announce that the kingdom of God was near. We do not have to claw our way to the center. We do not have to hurry and scramble to become big to prove our worth. Those who claim to be a people of faith must walk by faith and not by sight. When a church is large and powerful, its ministry bears witness to the power of the institution. But when a community is small and marginal and still chooses to turn outward and lavishly serve its neighbors, then its ministry bears witness to the power of Christ. It is another manifestation of the holy irony that surrounds Jesus. Only what is small and marginal can truly bear witness to the incomprehensibly comprehensive power of God. The goodness of God abounds in small, in the practice of humility, the presence of grace, and the experience of delight.

10

HUMILITY

The Church Should Not Be Excellent

MY PATERNAL GRANDMOTHER was the oldest of eleven children. Born in the heart of the Great Depression, her father died when she was thirteen years old, forcing my great-grandmother to make unbearable choices. She couldn't feed all her children, so she put my grandmother and her oldest son on a train to an orphanage. In later years, my great-grandmother remarried, but my grandmother never felt welcomed by her new stepfather. She chose to stay in the orphanage and never lived with her mother or siblings again.

My grandmother had a ferocious intellect and, with the encouragement of her beloved Aunt Myrtle, attended Berea College in Kentucky. Berea is a no-tuition liberal arts college. Every enrolled student is the beneficiary of a fully funded education. My grandmother knew she was incredibly fortunate to have the opportunity to earn a college degree. After graduation, she applied to the Columbia University Graduate School of Journalism. Assuming she had been accepted and awarded the necessary financial assistance, she got on a train to New York. Upon arrival, she presented herself at the dean's office, explaining that she had moved before she had received her acceptance letter. The dean explained that, in fact, they had not sent her an acceptance letter because she had not been accepted.

But, family lore goes, he was so impressed with what he termed her *spunk* that he arranged for her admittance and gave her the money she needed to buy her books. She graduated with a master's in journalism in 1941. That same year, she became a "girl reporter" for *The Courier-Journal* in Louisville.

My paternal grandfather worked part time as a copy editor at the paper while he studied engineering. The great secret of my grandfather's life was that he was adopted as an infant. The two of them married and vowed to raise children whose success would justify the faith of everyone who had ever invested in them: my grandfather's adoptive family, Aunt Myrtle, Berea College, the sympathetic dean of the journalism school, and the editors at *The Courier-Journal.* Everyone who had taken a chance on either of them would look at what they had become and know they had invested wisely.

My grandparents had something to prove to the world. They felt they had a debt to repay. And the way they would repay those who believed in them was to be excellent. They raised their children with the stories of their own childhoods, impressing upon them the importance of achieving excellence.

My father was their oldest child. During his first semester of college, he pledged a fraternity, discarded a biology major he found too challenging, and earned the "gentleman's C." He was quite content. My grandmother, however, was horrified. She wrote him a letter with a concluding line that has become a family legend: "If the horizon of your ambition is to become an affable insurance man, so be it. But we raised you to be something more."

My father got the message and adjusted his efforts accordingly. Average was unacceptable. Excellence was essential. He earned a law degree, worked for the Department of Justice, and excelled as a partner in a prestigious law firm. Over the course of his career, he earned numerous awards and distinctions. Everything about his life fulfilled his parents' vow.

My grandparents were blessed that people had seen them as worthy and given them opportunities. They sought to repay those who blessed them by being exceptional. And they were. As the firstborn of their firstborn, I grew up learning of my grandmother's pluck and courage. My sisters and I inherited a moral obligation to work hard and achieve excellence. We were Hazel's granddaughters. We could be anything we wanted when we grew up, anything at all—as long as we were excellent.

We could be anything except an affable insurance man. We owed it to her, and those who had believed in her, to be more than that.

I grew up proud of my grandmother and inspired by her story. In many ways, it served me well. It motivated me to work hard, to challenge myself, to dig deep. If anything, a call to ministry intensified my drive for excellence. After all, who was more worthy of excellence than Jesus? Others might be laboring for wealth or prestige or power, but I was laboring for the Savior of the cosmos. He was worthy of the longest hours, the deepest study, the finest programs, the most brilliant sermons and prayers and songs. How could I repay the glory of God with mediocrity?

However intensely people labored for themselves, I had to push harder. After all, hadn't the apostle Paul taught me that I could do all things through Christ who strengthened me?

If my family legacy demanded more of me than life as an affable insurance man, then how much more should I demand of myself to give to Christ? Underneath all my study and preparation and labor was the unspoken determination to be anything but an average pastor. For Christ's sake, for my grandmother's sake, I would be excellent.

I could preach a fierce sermon about unconditional grace. I earnestly encouraged and consoled any person seeking pastoral care that God loved and liked them just as they were. I taught children the first question and answer of the *Westminster Catechism*: "What is the chief end of humanity? To know God and enjoy God forever." I believed it for other people, but I was proud not to choose it for myself. In Christ, grace abounds. But as for me and my house, we would honor God by rejecting grace and choosing excellence.

And then God showed me a more excellent way.

* * *

I spent one of the most sacred nights of my life in the partially soiled bed of an addict. Shamefully, I didn't much care for the addict, but I adored her child. But that was good enough for her, because the addict also only cared about her child.

When members of our church realized that we were enabling the addiction and preventing recovery by pretending the addict didn't have a problem, I was part of the group who showed up for the intervention. It was horrible. To see the mother's delighted smile when she opened the door and saw us. To watch shame freeze that smile into a rictus grin as she realized what we had come to do. What had seemed unpleasant but righteous and necessary in the abstract now felt like a brutal attack—not just to her but to us. A moral gang jump "for her own good."

But it wasn't for her own good, really; it was for the good of the child. I can't speak for anyone else, but in my heart, I wasn't there for the mother. I didn't love her. I only cared about her as an accessory in her child's life. And I played that card brutally, when my "turn" came in the game of this intervention. "You're endangering the life of your child every day, every time you drive. You're stealing your kid's childhood. Each night your kid has to put you to bed, each time your kid has to clean up your sickness. You say you love your child, but love wouldn't do that."

It was true. It also was cruel. I think it was faithful. Maybe. I don't regret it. But still, I'm ashamed.

So after we'd bullied the mother into rehab, I was glad when they said to me that someone needed to stay with the child. We wanted to keep things as normal as possible, so we decided we'd take turns staying there in the apartment so that the child wouldn't have to live out of a suitcase or wake up in a strange place. And it was a balm to go out of my way, to be perceived as kind after I'd been so cruelly faithful.

So I showed up again, and we made dinner together, and played a card game afterward. I helped with homework and supervised bedtime. And then, it was time to sleep and I realized I didn't know where to go. The child told me, "You can sleep in my mom's bed." There were no extra sheets, no access to a washing machine and dryer. The bed was still unmade from the night before. But this child had already watched the mother's humiliating and raw intervention. I didn't want to reject the hospitality the child offered me out of their falling-apart world. So I slept in the addict's bed because I didn't want her child to wake up in the morning and find me in a chair and see that I thought the bed was defiled.

I laid down in that bed, and it smelled like stale cigarettes and cheap alcohol and misery. It smelled like the mother's love for her child, the kind of love that bears the unbearable without counting the cost.

I laid in the addict's bed and thought about how she was God knew where, also in an unfamiliar bed, alone and humiliated and in pain. And there were stains and smells and I was disgusted with myself because it was only then, wrapped in her misery, that I saw the sacred beauty of her life. To rise up each morning out of this bed and find the strength to pour cereal for the child, drive to school, hustle every day to find a way to make ends meet, and show up in church on Sunday to praise God for good report cards, to praise God for who the child was and could be, to praise God and ask nothing for herself. I saw the selflessness of navigating this much pain every day, a slow crucifixion of the spirit, to mother her child. I saw the glory in the mother's choice to do everything she could in the hope that the child would grow up strong and free and leave her behind.

Yes, we were right to do all we could to get the mother to rehab. But now, in hindsight, I know we should have stood in a circle and applauded her first. Because her suffering and weakness—which so deeply offended and frightened me—actually revealed the glory of God Almighty. We hadn't come there for her. We were there because we saw the promise of her child. We saw her as a liability, a defective who needed to be fixed, a threat her child needed to be protected from. And lying in her bed that night, I understood that she saw herself the same way. And I wept, from the beauty and the shame.

We live in a world where some people matter and some people don't. Where a few are seen to have promise, but most aren't seen at all. We live in a world where we treasure the young for their potential but despise and reject them when they grow up because they disappoint us.

And out of this world we build our churches, so even followers of Jesus believe it is natural to circle around in love to protect a child but then circle back in self-righteousness to shame an adult. We do both in the name of goodness. But the unclean bed of an addict becomes an altar when the Spirit impresses upon you the glory-weight of her sacrificial love for her child.

I didn't understand how or why, but I knew sleeping in that bed was sacred that night. I knew that, if I let it, it could teach me more about Christ than any theology class ever would.

On the cross we see love defeated, love humiliated, love shamed and in pain, love with loose bowels and blood that stains, love that cries out in agony and despair. And we see, still, in all of that, love holds on for the beloved. On the cross we see love that endures what can't be endured for as long as it can, love strong enough to absorb agony without passing it along. This is a love that requires us to bear witness to its suffering but doesn't require us to suffer. This is love in pain refusing to hide. At the cross we see that love unwilling to suffer any pain isn't love at all. Until I laid down and closed my eyes in an addict's bed, I couldn't see any of that.

Jesus looked down from the cross to care for his mother. And I slept in the bed of a mother who endured the crucifixion of addiction every day, who still rose up each morning to care for her child. Resurrection does not glorify suffering, but it does vindicate a love deep and powerful enough to endure suffering for the salvation of the beloved.

Christians like me believe that Jesus is the Son of God, the perfect essence of the divine in human flesh. And while he walked on earth, Jesus accomplished incredible feats. He walked on water, he cast out demons, he multiplied loaves and fishes to feed crowds, he raised the dead, he challenged all the sacred experts. I could go on and on, but suffice it to say, everywhere he went was miracle city.

And we believers look at that and think, "Wow. I want to be like that." And so we try with all our might to be excellent. Maybe we can't be perfect, but we can be excellent. Jesus was perfect, so we should be excellent. Most of us can't work miracles, but we can try to build the biggest buildings and attract the largest crowds and succeed at the most successful successes. Or we can relentlessly beat ourselves up when we don't; the least we can do is that. And anything that isn't impressive, we can hide and reject and deny. Because Jesus deserves nothing less than our very best, doesn't he? Jesus did all that water walking and storm calming and feeding and healing and teaching and exorcising of demons for us, so the least we can do is be the very most excellent humans for him. Right?

But the thing is, every excellent thing that Jesus did, all the miracles and wonders, even the raising people from the dead: They were reruns. Patriarchs and prophets did all that before. Moses parted the waters and called down the plagues and made a water fountain out of a rock. Joshua made the sun stand still. Elijah multiplied flour and oil to feed a starving family, and Elisha raised the widow's son. (Or maybe it was the other way around. I always get those guys mixed up.) The point is, before Jesus, other miracle workers walked the earth. So Jesus's exceptionalism wasn't in his excellence.

The only thing that Jesus did in the name of God that no one had done before was set aside his every advantage and absorb cruel violence. His exceptional act was to endure crucifixion, a death of pain and public humiliation and, in doing so, bear witness to a glorious goodness that cannot be shamed or destroyed. The exceptionalism of Jesus wasn't in the kind of powerful, impressive life we aspire to have; it doesn't look like the excellence we fetishize. Jesus did not overcome. For love's sake, he endured—until he didn't.

And that's a story you can't hear in the sermon of a powerful preacher behind a shiny pulpit. It's the truth you absorb in the stiff, sweat-soaked bedsheets of an addict determined to hang on for her kid.

Culture, at least in the West, tells us to be excellent or be ashamed, to overcome our adversities or quietly succumb to them without making a fuss, to love those who inspire us and despise those who fail to meet our expectations. But in the kingdom, we are free to be frail and failing humans who are sanctified when they discover their God-given worth has never been at stake. There has never been anything to prove. There is no debt to be repaid by achievement. And many will reject this kind of glory. Believing a sanctification that includes all humans is worthless, they will turn and walk proudly away. They will build their mansions and practice hustle culture in the outer darkness where there is the weeping and gnashing of teeth that fuels the pursuit of excellence.

I learned about excellence first in my grandmother's story. I began to unlearn that kind of excellence the night I slept in the addict's bed. And then, because God has an offensively direct sense of humor, I bore witness to the embodiment of the more excellent way when I became the pastor of a disciple of Jesus Christ named David Hicks.

* * *

If you ask anyone who knew David, they'll tell you he was a humble and sincere follower of Jesus. Even if they don't believe in Jesus, they'll tell you that. Because no matter what you believe, if you spent any time with David, you knew for sure what he believed—and not because he told you about Jesus but because of his extraordinary posture toward the world. The man radiated kindness.

As a young man, David served overseas and in combat as a naval officer. He came home and started his own business and threw himself into serving his community. He spent all his free time volunteering. Officially, he served at the church, Habitat for Humanity, and as a Scoutmaster hiking and hauling tents and helping young men earn their Eagle Scout Awards. Unofficially, David was always ready to help his neighbors navigate whatever was difficult, whatever was unpleasant, whatever was tedious and uncelebrated. David was ever ready to do whatever he could do to make someone else's life easier. If you had a flat tire or needed something hauled to the dump or a ride to a doctor's appointment, you called David. Whatever needed doing, David did it, with a glad sincerity, preferably anonymously. But people couldn't help but tell the stories of his kindness.

By the time I met him, David was in his seventies. He was a frail man by then, very thin and slightly stooped. He shuffled when he walked. I found myself holding my breath when I followed him down a sidewalk or a hallway. He looked as though a gentle wind would blow him over. When he spoke, it was soft and slow and you had to lean over to listen. But no matter how restless and in a hurry you were, you did. Because you couldn't rush past David's kindness. It made you turn aside. It made you want to take off your shoes. I don't know how else to say it—just that the man exuded goodness at a frequency that was palpable.

David's kindness made you uncomfortably aware of every sarcastic comment, every snide aside, every self-centered choice you'd ever made. Because here he was, living proof that gentleness, patience, and self-control were possible, for those who wished to cultivate them. David was kind not to some or most but to all. It wasn't his personality; it was the embodied expression of values he'd pursued for a lifetime.

Therapists have coined the term *unconditional positive regard* to describe the expression of empathy, acceptance, and support to someone regardless of what they say or do. Unconditional positive regard is essential in a therapeutic setting, because no one can risk honesty, vulnerability, or change without an unshakable sense of safety and belonging. The Hebrew word for this is *chesed*: the steadfast kindness of God toward God's people. God shows chesed toward creation and toward the people. God is, as the refrain goes, "compassionate and gracious, slow to anger and abounding in mercy" (Exod 34; Ps 86:15, 103:8, 145:8–9). Chesed was what differentiated God from idols.

God's chesed was expressed not in proportion to the people's goodness but in proportion to God's goodness—which is to say, wholly and completely and constantly. David Hicks wasn't stupid, and he wasn't naive. He knew many people were likely to see his kindness as weakness and believe they were taking advantage of him. He had opinions and preferences, good days and bad days like everyone else, but he was steadfastly kind through it all. His posture of chesed toward the world mirrored God's own.

When I was new in my congregation, I had the opportunity to speak publicly in favor of marriage equality. This was, shamefully, still quite controversial at the time, and I wondered, only three months into this call, if this might cause the church to quietly send me on my way. A few days after I spoke in support of full inclusion of LGBTQIA+ siblings in our denomination, I was walking to my car and heard David call me, faintly, from across the parking lot. I saw that he was coming toward me and I waited. I didn't know David well yet, but he was an elderly, white, Southern businessman, so I was pretty sure I knew what was coming.

I was wrong.

He said he made up his mind about homosexuality when he toured the Holocaust Memorial Museum in Washington, D.C. He told me that was when he learned that it wasn't just Jewish people but also gay people, people who were disabled or neurodivergent, and Romani peoples who were incarcerated and murdered in concentration camps. David paused and looked down. Then he looked up at me and said, "I decided then and there that whoever Hitler was against, I was going to be for. I want our church to be a safe and welcoming place for everyone."

And he made it so. Each Sunday, David stood at the front door of our church, waiting to welcome every person who came to worship. As a congregation, we are notoriously loose about arrival times, which means that many Sundays he stood out there keeping watch for close to half the service. He didn't want anyone to come in without being welcomed.

As the church began to grow and change, we welcomed a family whose oldest son was a tall, nonverbal, autistic, Black man in his early thirties named Jason. Jason made it known that he wanted to serve the church, so David invited him to join him in the greeting ministry. For years, the two of them waited at the threshold of the sanctuary every Sunday, scanning the horizon, watching and waiting for the ones they could welcome. After the end of the first hymn, they would come inside, Jason leading David by the hand across the front of the sanctuary to his pew. Those with eyes to see saw the kingdom in our midst.

When an amyotrophic lateral sclerosis (ALS) diagnosis made it impossible for David to drive, he tried to give his truck away to a single mother in the congregation. Then he began to ride the bus every day from his home on the east side of the city to his office in the center of the city. It took him more than two hours every morning and every evening. He invested that time. He set about befriending everyone he met on the bus. Once he learned their name, he'd invite them to worship. He'd promise them he'd be waiting for them on the front step. To my knowledge, no one he met on the bus ever came, but David was undeterred. He kept inviting, he kept standing on the threshold, waiting to welcome.

David's world kept getting smaller and smaller. When his disease progressed so that he could no longer stand, David reluctantly took a seat in the pews. Very soon a day came when he could no longer do even that. He became homebound and began to use a wheelchair. And that's when he asked his wife, Libba, to please take the bench away from their upright piano. He had stopped taking piano lessons before he finished elementary school, but he wheeled himself over and began to reteach himself to play. Eighty-nine years old and in the end stages of ALS, he decided it was time to make music again because it was something beautiful he could still do. One last gift of chesed he could offer a jaded and cynical world. His wife made a video recording and sent it to the church, and we played it during Christmas Eve worship. He died seven days later.

I spent my undergraduate days as the least talented student in the school of music, stubbornly refusing to quit. I learned the hard way that excellence can be quantified and people can be ranked according to the proportion of it they possess. Excellence is exclusive and impressive. Experts teach it. Students aspire to achieve it. It is performed in concert halls, it sells out stadiums, and it wins competitions. Excellence can be monetized. David's music was the opposite of excellent, according to the experts. And yet it was one of the most profoundly sacred sounds I've ever had the privilege to hear.

By my grandmother's trauma-formed definition, David was not excellent. When he died, he was not wealthy. He was not powerful. As far as I know, he was not a leader in his industry (although, if he had been, he'd certainly never have let me or anyone else know). He chose not to pursue those things.

The Sunday after he died, I asked everyone in the congregation to stand up if David was the first person who ever welcomed them to the church. Almost everyone in the sanctuary rose to their feet. In that moment we saw that this life together, which meant so much to us all, had been stitched together by David's kindness. Maybe David wasn't many of the things this warped world calls excellent. But this world is lousy with such excellence, and that hasn't made it more closely resemble the kingdom of heaven. Maybe there are enough people fighting to be the most excellent of whatever they are. Those who were welcomed by David are now welcomers, and that's revolutionary.

The church of Jesus Christ should not be excellent, not as this fallen world defines it. We are called to the small way of chesed. So we cherish all people, especially those the world judges to be small, worthless, and lacking potential. And the church sings out to those who are exhausted from trying to prove themselves worthy that "there is a more excellent way," and invites them to lay down their ceaseless striving and rest and flourish in a new identity as Christ's beloved ones. Freed from the unachievable burden of earning and maintaining cultural excellence, we can seek out those who are being crushed by pain and failure and encircle them in a ring of chesed and belonging.

David was something better than excellent. And at the end of his life, when disease took almost every power he had, he defied all the loss and pain to begin again, learning anew to make something beautiful.

Oh, and one other thing. You might not believe me, but I swear I'm not making this up. David was an insurance man. The most extraordinary and faithful disciple of Jesus Christ I've ever known also happened to be an affable insurance man. May his tribe increase.

11

GRACE

The Bread Will Rise

JESUS WAS A revolutionary but not in packaging we recognize. Like all revolutionaries, he came to tell us another way is possible, that everything familiar must pass away. He called us to repent: to turn away from what we know and head toward what we could not know, which is the kingdom of God. He came showing and telling us not that it was coming, in the future, but that it was already at hand. It was near, not just chronologically but also geographically.

The kingdom of heaven entered into history with the birth of the Messiah and began offering citizenship to spiritual refugees with the inauguration of his ministry. Anyone righteous, foolish, or desperate enough to leave behind all they knew, cross the wild seas of unknowing and unlearning, and enter into a new and unfamiliar way of being is always welcomed in. All who inexplicably choose to follow him when he says "come and see" discover that though his way often feels like death, it is, in fact, the way of abundant life.

The kingdom of heaven he calls us to is everywhere and nowhere, both invisible and inescapable. Without permission or pedigree, without an army or recognizable authority, he declared that his unperceivable kingdom was already present and that all other visible structures and hierarchies were rapidly passing away. The evidence to the contrary is so strong that for generations, even the most devout followers modified his message to make it more reasonable.

When Jesus said the kingdom of God was near, we earnestly explain, he didn't mean the kingdom was near *here*; he meant it was coming soon. We've turned Jesus's announcement into a prediction. We've twisted it into a future-oriented metaphor. We soberly explain that Jesus had to have meant something other than what he said because, well, *look at this place.*

We are certain that "the kingdom of God is near" and its extraordinary cousin, "the kingdom of God is in the midst of you," must be metaphors or promises, because the words make no sense to us any other way. We are all too familiar with the ruling structures of our world. Then and now, people trying to follow Jesus live in the real world. We understand how governing and authority work, and when we look around for evidence that a good and loving God has suddenly assumed control, we don't find much.

We recognize the kingdoms of the world by the way they express their power and authority. Across millennia, this remains constant. Pharoah's Egypt waged war to make peace, enslaved people deemed unworthy of freedom and full humanity, collected taxes, built roads, and codified rights and privileges. Caesar's Roman Empire waged war to make peace, enslaved people deemed unworthy of freedom and full humanity, collected taxes, built roads, and codified rights and privileges. The American government wages war to make peace, enslaves people deemed unworthy of freedom and full humanity, collects taxes, builds roads, and codifies rights and privileges.

Those bold and foolish enough to take Jesus at his word reject the premise that Jesus's promises are metaphors. They question them: "Where, exactly, is the kingdom of God? These other kingdoms and governments and authorities seem mighty real to me. Show me the power and presence of the kingdom of heaven. Where is its authority? What are its laws and culture? Show me its institutions, its influence, its force, its provision." The boldest and most faithful among us will hear Jesus's announcement and demand holy proof: "If the kingdom of God is here, show us, Lord! What is it like? How can we recognize it?"

Jesus answered these questions with his shortest parable of all: "The kingdom of heaven is like leaven that a woman took and mixed through 60 pounds of flour until it had worked through all the dough" (Matt 13:33; my translation).

Jesus says the kingdom of God is like leaven. Most contemporary English translations use the more familiar term: *yeast*. But yeast and leaven are not precisely the same thing. We buy our Fleischmann's active yeast in the little packets or brown glass jars we find in the baking aisle. We break the seal and measure out dry, crumbly pellets into our mixing bowls.

But biblical leaven was unprocessed, typically a small lump of old bread or dough carefully preserved, organically containing both the yeast and the lactic acid bacteria necessary to make bread rise. Mixed into the new dough, a piece of the old bread seeds the new.

Jesus's revelation that the kingdom of heaven was like yeast or leaven would have shocked his original audience, because the biblical record suggests that God was not a big fan of leavened bread. In Exodus, God forbids the people to make an offering of "anything containing yeast to me" (Exod 23:18; my translation). In Leviticus, God specifies that grain offerings people bring to the altar must be made with salt but without yeast. God was so serious about this that the prohibitions are repeated in Leviticus 6:17 and Exodus 34:25. Given the expense and vulnerability of biblical scrolls, any repetition in Scripture is highly significant. Why does God insist so adamantly on unleavened bread? What is God's issue with yeast?

Bread was a dietary staple in the ancient Near East. Scholars estimate bread made up 50 to 75 percent of the average person's daily caloric intake. People ate bread all day, every day, and most of it was leavened. And yet the bread set aside to be offered to God, the holy bread, had to be unleavened. Ancient scribes and rabbis searched for the meaning of this exception and concluded that leaven was inconsistent with the concept of the perfect, unchangeable holiness of God because leaven was an agent of change, one that altered and transformed the component parts of dough. Those seeking to make an offering "pleasing to the Lord" were instructed to give the best: the very first, perfect fruits of the harvest; young, pure, and unblemished animals. Stipulations that bread offerings be unleavened were consistent with God's preference for gifts that were unaltered: pure and uncontaminated. Furthermore, the dominant, though not universal, strain of rabbinic thought associated leaven with decay and corruption.

Biologically, they weren't wrong, because the active component of leaven is yeast. Yeast is a single-celled organism, one of about 144,000 known species of the fungi kingdom, along with rusts, smuts, mildews, molds, and mushrooms. Like all fungus, yeast feed on simple, soluble nutrients like sugars and amino acids. Even in a hostile environment, one without adequate nutrients, yeast have unique genetic adaptations that, when triggered by stress, allow them to exist in a sort of suspended animation. They are found literally everywhere. If it's not sterile, there are yeast on it. Yeast are omnipresent. They are on the tips of your fingers, the type on this page, inside the infinitesimal tear in your skin, and wafting invisibly through the air.

But yeast cells don't start to grow and multiply until the environment around them begins to decay. Then they feed, converting the inert sugars of no-longer-living things into energy. So when a piece of fruit falls to the ground and dies, the yeast around it flares into life. Yeast are decomposers; they thrive when everything around them begins to decay. No wonder priests and rabbis found leaven spiritually unpalatable.

Yeast literally feed on death, dismantling what once was living into component parts and consuming it.

* * *

You might be trying to stay awake, wondering what any of this biology lesson has to do with faith. But when Jesus began talking about *leaven*, his original audience would have been on familiar ground. They wouldn't have been surprised to hear leaven talk in the middle of theology class, because the Hebrew people always understood their relationship with leaven as an expression of their life with God. For generations, ritual practices surrounding leaven were a core way the people passed down their spiritual origin story. People believed leavened bread had the power to desecrate holy spaces. The presence of leavened bread on the holy altar was corrosive and unpleasing to the Lord. In sacred space and stories, yeast was inextricably associated with the terrible and omnipresent powers of death and decay—and empire.

Here's why: The night before God miraculously liberated the Hebrew people from Egyptian slavery, God gave them a detailed list of preparations. Before their journey to freedom, the people were to sacrifice a lamb and spread its blood on the lintel of their doorway so that the plague of death, which would secure their new life, would pass over their homes without harming anyone inside. The plague would not pass over the homes unmarked by the blood of the lamb but instead enter in and claim the life of every firstborn son.

After marking the thresholds of their homes, God instructed the people to prepare a meal from the sacrificed lamb but warned them to eat it in haste with their sandals on their feet and their tunics tucked into their belts. God also told them liberation was so close that there was not time to wait for their bread to rise. So they would have to bake and eat it unleavened. The first ritual feast anticipating their liberation would be yeast-free. Each year thereafter, the people would prepare to celebrate the anniversary of the Passover with a great unleavening: ritually ridding their homes of yeast for seven days. Then, at the annual Passover feast, they would eat unleavened bread and remember the story of their salvation. In this way, they would consume, both physically and spiritually, the story of God delivering their ancestors from oppression. The primary spiritual significance of unleavened bread was that it helped people recall the speed with which liberation came, when it finally came.

But I wonder, given the biological and theological association of yeast with decay and corruption, given its prohibition in Temple offerings, if there isn't another layer of meaning as well. Remember, biblical leaven is just a lump of bread or dough set aside to seed the next batch.

Many fermented foods have this kind of starter. You need a mother to start yogurt, a mini wort for beer, brine for pickling cucumbers. Starters are the catalyst of the fermentation process. They are essential, not just for making bread but also for cheese, kimchi, sauerkraut, kombucha, and other foods. And there is a term describing the category of starters which initiate the fermentation process: culture.

The word culture comes from the Latin word *cultura*, derivative of *colere*, which means "to cultivate." There are layers of meaning here. Literally, culture is the way the raw materials of creation—land and creatures and life—are altered and manipulated. Biologically, a culture is a community of bacteria and fungi that transform their environment. Anthropologically, culture is the way humans live and make meaning in community: our customs, rituals, stories, laws, totems, and taboos.

Follow the etymological trail even further back and you get to the Indo-European root word *kwel*, meaning "to revolve," from which we derive the words *cycle*, *circle*, and *culture*. The word culture can describe both the cyclical ongoing process of fermentation and the stories, knowledge, and practices passed down from one generation to another. Culture is what we return to again and again to shape our lives.

The message of Scripture, from beginning to end, is the story of God entering into human history. The origin of the peculiar relationship between the Hebrew people, their yeast, and their God happened at a specific place and time. The story of Exodus is the story of God freeing a particular people from their suffering and the oppression created by a particular culture.

The Hebrew people were enslaved by an empire whose economy required the raw materials of human misery and desperation. Pharaoh maintained his power by inequitably distributing what was produced by the labor of a vast class of powerless and suffering people. Pharaoh mandated harsh labor, which consumed and ruined Hebrew bodies. And when, despite their cruel oppression, the Hebrew community continued to grow and thrive, Pharaoh grew fearful of their strength, the very strength upon which he profited. He feared vengeance. He worried that those he oppressed would rise up and seek to destroy the one who was destroying them. He traded in violence, so he expected violence, and he moved to protect himself by unleashing more brutality upon the people. He decreed that all their sons should be murdered at birth. This is the contagion of violence. Pharoah used the only force he knew, the power to kill, to protect himself. He sought to put their future to death. Pharaoh's imperial power demanded the blood of Hebrew baby boys. Egyptian imperial culture ran on the fuel of ruined bodies, violence, and the threat of death. Spoiler alert—the United States of America runs on the same imperial fuel.

God entered into this history to disrupt it. God interrupted the cycles of violence and oppression by freeing the Hebrew people. God liberated them not from a place but from a culture of death. Once liberated, the Hebrew people would fulfill the divine promise to their ancestor Abraham. They would live free in the promised land, and through them, all nations would be blessed.

But not if the culture in the promised land replicated the culture of Pharoah's Egypt. If the chosen people also built a culture with an economy based on the raw materials of human misery, suffering, and oppression—if they took the leaven of Egypt with them into Canaan—they would remain enslaved. So God prohibited the people from taking any of that yeast—none of that culture—with them on the wilderness path to freedom. In the absence of the leaven and culture of Egypt, the people would have the chance to forge a new relationship with power and death.

* * *

Given all this sacred history and theology, it was extraordinary when Jesus informed those first skeptical seekers that the kingdom of God was like leaven. It wasn't surprising that his kingdom of heaven sermons included a discussion of leaven. The people already had a theological relationship with leavened bread. But Jesus was speaking to people who, for generations, had carefully limited and controlled their use of yeast, who saw the nature of yeast as incompatible with the nature of God. In sacred space and stories, yeast was inextricably associated with the terrible and omnipresent powers of empire, death, and decay. So the crowd would have expected to hear how *un*-leaven-like God's kingdom was. But Jesus says just the opposite.

Now, Jesus was declaring, the great reversal has begun. God's realm could not be infected by death or decay. In fact, the opposite is happening. The holy grace of God is corrupting the profane. With the incarnation, the undiluted holiness of grace has been mixed back into the measure of creation. In the former days, leaven was a symbol of the explosive power of death and decay, its mere presence believed powerful enough to desecrate the holy. But in the new realm, it is the sacred that has become infectious. Now it is grace, at work in the world like leaven, infusing and transforming all it encounters, even the forces of destruction and death. The kingdom is already in our midst like leaven, and with it, Jesus says, comes a new culture of abundant life.

When Jesus revealed that the kingdom of heaven was like leaven transforming inert flour into risen bread, he was giving them eyes to see the nature of grace in his kingdom. Most of us learned that grace is simply the willingness of God to forgive the unforgivable, and who among us would dare to expect more than that from God? But what if there is even more to grace? What if God is able not only to forgive the unforgivable but also to enter into the suffering and destruction our violent culture has unleashed and, in turn, bring it back to life? What if the resurrection wasn't just reserved for the body of Christ but has now been unleashed upon us all? What if in Jesus we see that, like leaven, God's grace could not be contained? It did not need to be protected from death. It would alter (and make an altar) of all it encountered. Human authorities could not harness power in the kingdom; no longer could the holy be corrupted by fear or greed.

And now we can begin to imagine a new culture of holiness, leavened by grace, that is truly good news for all people. Now the power to kill, oppress, or destroy is no longer ultimate. The kingdom is in our midst and a plague of healing has been unleashed: its symptoms are freedom and new life. Like leaven, the kingdom of grace spreads and transforms. This news is so breathtakingly good we can scarcely take it in.

* * *

You don't need a packet of yeast from the store (or a lump of yesterday's dough) to make bread. Without either, you can still make risen bread. You just need a new culture, what bakers and brewers call a starter.

And the wonder of it all is how extraordinarily simple it is to make a new starter. You put water and something organic in an unsealed container. You can use almost anything: grapes, figs, acorns, hulled wheat. And then you wait. The bacteria you need is already invisibly there. Wild yeast is wafting on every current of the wind. In only a few days, the fruit will begin to dissolve, its color leaching into the water. And then, if you look closely into the opaque water, you'll see bubbles on the surface. And that's how you'll know they are there. Power-filled microscopic yeast are there, growing and turning the sugars of the decaying matter back into life.

If you put grapes into your water, you'll be on your way to wine. If you take the right amount of that starter and mix it with flour, you'll get dough, and if you cover it, it will rise. How will you know? You'll have to try and see. Or maybe seek out the wisdom of one who already knows. Sit at her feet as she does this again and again. Come and see. The bread will rise.

Western Christianity has gotten the kingdom of God violently, tragically, and blasphemously wrong. For all that we claim to be biblical literalists, we weren't listening when Jesus told us his kingdom would come like a woman working leaven through dough. We looked around and saw the dominance of empires and the power of the cultures of scarcity, violence, and death. We imagined God was at work transforming and harnessing that culture for goodness' sake. We couldn't imagine any other kind of power except the power to kill and destroy anything that would not yield. We couldn't imagine a kingdom built by nourishing and not bloodshed. But the good news of the gospel is that, anticipated or not, understood or not, the kingdom of heaven comes like leaven, and it displaces human cultures of violent imperialism. The leaven of the old culture must be cast out. The new leaven of the culture of shalom has come. Before we can believe it, we must imagine it.

Perhaps now is the time for another great unleavening. When so many are exhausted and confused, when so many have walked away from faith that once nurtured and gave life meaning, when so many have been banned from sanctuaries that claim to have sole distribution rights of the holy—perhaps it is time for us to clean out long-neglected theological cupboards and discard leaven that never should have found a place there.

Our culture's ideas of excellence and efficiency, power and scarcity have invaded and shaped our common life, so perhaps this breakdown is ultimately a gift. How many times have we seen the voices and preferences of the powerful drown out the cries of the weak and rejected, knowing it was wrong but mistakenly accepting it as inevitable? How often have we grieved deep brokenness in our community but decided it was not possible or prudent to get involved? How often have we overlooked the ways white supremacy, patriarchy, and heteronormativity shape life in the church with the same brutality they shape life outside of it? Just because we can't imagine any other way to be the church doesn't mean there isn't one.

We are surrounded by wild and holy yeast. The kingdom of God has been initiated in Jesus. He is the starter. He is the culture. He is the leaven. He has entered into our life of corruption and decay. He has entered fully in, holding himself back from nothing, not even death. Entering death, he has dismantled it into its component pieces, fermenting and fomenting life, even at the grave. He is risen. He is the bread of life. The power of life has overcome and absorbed all things, even death itself.

So perhaps we can use the words of Jesus as our new starter. What would it look like to grow the church's common life from the culture of Jesus? Would we stop telling polite lies and learn to sit with uncomfortable truths about our individual and communal complicity with sin? Would we listen to Jesus's parable about the fool who built bigger barns, and begin to question the faithfulness of large endowments? Would we hear the story of Jesus feeding the five thousand out of the offering of one child's five loaves and two fish and begin to question our learned helplessness? Would we let Jesus's stories about prodigal sons and Good Samaritans reshape our understanding of what it means to be a good neighbor? Would we learn, finally, how to be faithful even when the world doesn't center or celebrate us?

* * *

One last brief science lesson: We've talked about the biology of fermentation but now the chemistry. The process of fermentation releases carbon dioxide and ethanol. Ethanol (ethyl alcohol) is the scientific name for alcohol. The presence of ethanol, which is produced when grapes start to ferment, transforms grape juice into red wine. Carbon dioxide is gas; it's what forms the bubbles in risen bread.

On the night he was betrayed, Jesus gathered with his friends to celebrate the Passover and eat unleavened bread. Later that night, the beautiful community that had formed around him would fray and dissolve into fear and lies. Later that night, Jesus allowed himself to be delivered over to captivity and death. But first, knowing all that lay before him, Jesus gathered his community around the table to remember God's liberation of their ancestors and to rejoice, once again, in their deliverance from the tenth plague of death.

And at the end of the liturgy, Jesus told his friends the time had come for him to die. Then he held up bread and wine and told them that his death would bring universal life. His death would redeem and transform all creation, becoming for them the bread of life and the cup of salvation. Jesus, our new leaven, the culture of the kingdom, making the bread of life and the cup of salvation, transforming death into new life.

This is a beautiful metaphor. It is also plain truth, clean as a bone. The narrow way that feels like death leads us to life. The way to find the kingdom is to know the wild yeast of God's grace is omnipresent. Undomesticated grace is all around us, so we learn to look for tiny bubbles on the surface that signal something so small as to be invisible is at work, making things new.

These bubbles are the prayers for your neighbor you lift up each night as you wait for sleep. They are the deep breaths you take trying to stay present and open as you seek understanding in conflict. They are the tears you shed as you listen to someone share their pain, the strength it takes to bear witness. They are formed in the awkward conversation you make as you seek forgiveness when you've wronged someone and also in the painful conversations when you seek to make peace with one who has wronged you. These bubbles signaling grace at work arise out of the times you show up because you've promised even though you are sure it won't make a difference. They rise also when you tell the truth that you are tired and spent and have no more to give. They are in the words of sincere thankfulness and encouragement you speak and in the stunned silence you create when you address offensive speech directly. They are fomented in the waters you trouble when you speak the truth no one is prepared to hear.

If you have eyes to see, you'll recognize the bubbles of new life rising up from sincere questions, brave doubts, and unsatisfying answers. These minuscule bubbles signal that grace is at work beneath the surface, sanctifying and calling forth life. Like leaven, grace is not something we produce or control. It is a force we cannot see or create. But like an experienced baker, we can learn to depend on it. When we yield to it, it transforms us. Consuming the death in us, by its power we are made new in Christ.

It is essential that those who follow Jesus understand and embrace the parable of the leaven. When we do not understand how the kingdom of God is already in our midst, we take it upon ourselves to recolonize creation for Christ as seems best in our own eyes. Ignorant of the power of leaven, we mistakenly believe God desires us to dominate and destroy those we see as evil or obstacles. Too fearful to trust what we cannot see, we misinterpret the call to take up our cross as a command to shoulder the responsibility of redemption. Without an understanding and embracing of the culture of the kingdom, our false understanding of the holy destroys us or makes us destroyers.

The revelation of Christ's kingdom doesn't call us to become proxy saviors or faux redeemers, but wise ones who have learned to live dependent upon the power of grace, like a seasoned baker who knows how to mix yeast into vast measures of flour, who has learned to trust the transforming power of a very little, who has learned exactly how long to wait to allow the bread to rise. We understand we are called not to save but to nourish and create. We rejoice and rest, knowing that God has given us everything we need to be faithful.

This is another reason why there is no shame in being small, and why we don't need to fear being invisible. We understand that we will appear powerless to those who can only see the power to dominate or control. We will appear foolish to those who believe in the power to take and not the power to give. But we have been freed by our understanding that the kingdom isn't something we build, but something the Holy Spirit ferments in us. We are no longer afraid of our own brokenness, sin, and weakness, for we know that our flourishing salvation comes from the power of God, which is not contingent upon the power of self. Grace is best understood as holy yeast, something that is in us but not of us, making out of all of us something more than we naturally are, bringing life even out of death. And not just life but abundant life, complete with wine and newly risen bread.

Wild yeast is the grace of God, decomposing death, reducing and restoring it to its component parts: life and eternity. God works her leaven into vast measures of flour, knowing life will rise and it will be abundant. God, who told us from the beginning, her name is "I will be who I will be." Sit at her feet as she does this again and again. Come and see. The bread will rise.

12

DELIGHT

Unless You Become Like a Child

I LOVE SUMMER camps. Each has its own ecosystem of rituals and traditions, chants and songs, challenges and awards. These ephemeral communities are catalysts of growth and change and becoming. Campers are children, and they enter in as such. They come to grow. I've seen children bloom into entirely new versions of themselves in these set-apart times of unconditional belonging. Summer camps and conferences give brave kids and wise adults the chance to try on a different way of living, with different values and different goals. They can be like the gospel sprung off the page.

For years, I was involved with an incredible, transformative Christian camp. Each day began with a raucous and joyful time of worship. The kids gathered around a playful interactive retelling of a Bible story and then responded with a cycle of cheers and chants and songs of various levels of beauty and silliness. Like all good worship, the takeaway is that you are part of this sacred story, you belong here, and nothing is required of you other than to enjoy the sacred goodness of being alive. Each day the camp invited an adult from the community and set aside a moment for the guest to share a short reading or devotional with the children. This practice showed the kids that people they didn't even know cared enough about them to travel to where the kids were and share something they loved. It's a hint about the kingdom of God, that the kind of community and belonging they find at the camp extends far beyond its temporal and geographical borders. There are other people like them, hiding in their grown-up suits.

At the end of each guest's visit, the kids sang a song to the adults, thanking them for the gift of their time and story and ending with a playful invitation encouraging the presenter to dance before the Lord. Part of the glee for the children was to see these adults—pastors, lawyers, judges, teachers, and principals—"strut their stuff" with glorious awkwardness, setting aside their dignity to enter into the joyful abandon of the camp community.

Some adults threw themselves into it and freestyled some incredible moves. Most clumsily and uncomfortably swayed back and forth. Either way, the tradition was a gift to the children. The sight of the respectable grown-ups dancing gave the kids a chance to be inspired or to take a turn being the expert, leading and encouraging their elders in the dance. The song encouraged a grown-up to do what came naturally to a carefree child on a summer morning.

And then one year I came back, and the ritual had been modified. The adult guests still came every day, but the kids' song with the invitation to dance had been cut. When I asked why, I was told that a major donor had complained. This person had been a guest during a morning worship service the previous summer and had been incredibly uncomfortable when he was invited to dance. He left complaining, "I didn't work this hard to come and hop around in front of a bunch of kids." Fearful that they would lose more essential donors, the camp removed the song. The takeaway was clear: Some people are too important to dance, especially in front of children.

When I was in seminary, I once pulled a book off a shelf about the theology of play. I tried to read the introduction, but I couldn't make sense of it. The author kept talking about *play*, but I couldn't figure out what they meant by the word. I kept looking for a special definition explaining an arcane meaning of the word that was unfamiliar to me. I knew what play was, of course. But as a young, serious seminary student, I didn't know what it was doing in a theology text. Play was silly. Play was for children. Play was what you did until you had the capacity to do anything that mattered. The cognitive dissonance was insurmountable. I put the book back on the shelf and walked away with holy dignity intact.

Jesus announced that the kingdom of God is near and that he is the narrow way into it. Then he pulled a child from the edges into the center of the circle and revealed the catch: You must change and become like this child if you want to enter in. Jesus invited us to enter the kingdom but like a child. I've heard one million metaphorical sermons on this text. Sermons about pride and human rights and universal childcare and everything else except the plain unnuanced truth of the teaching. Jesus isn't telling us to care for children (though he surely is in favor of this). He is telling us to learn something essential from them. He is telling us that we must become like them.

We don't know what this means, but even so, it's still a dealbreaker for many of us. We are committed to Jesus, and we are committed to our self-selected role in his kingdom. "Let my sons sit on your right and left hand, Jesus," a mother begs for her sons. "You know not what you ask for," he answers. You can't teach someone something they are confident they already know.

Oh, we know, Jesus. We know everything about your kingdom and our place in it. You don't need to tell us anything. We know exactly who we want to be. We will be the architects, designers, and builders. We will run the marketing campaign and call it evangelism. We will run security and call it discipleship. We will be C-suite directors and managers and distributors. We will be the experts. Don't worry, we will be patient and benign experts. We will smile indulgently as we carefully and decisively administer grace. We will be little Christs. We will be your proxy anointed ones. We will do important and salvific work with great competency. People will rise up and call us blessed.

Jesus said the greatest in the kingdom would be servants of all, and it takes some creativity, but we can make that one work for us. We are down to serve, ceaselessly and publicly, like our patron saint Martha. It's not the serving that causes us to back away slowly. It's the call to childlikeness. Who are we without our dignity and competency and control? Why would anyone want to live like that? Like a child? An unselfconscious, awkwardly dancing, make-yourself-small child? Is there no other way?

* * *

My friend and colleague Sarah is married to a very tall man who is also a pastor. I've never asked, but Mark must be nine-and-a-half feet tall. Sarah and I became close when we were both serving as suburban youth ministers in Charlotte. For several years, we collaborated with other Presbyterian congregations to host a community-wide weekend retreat for teenagers. We gathered more than two hundred middle and high school students and over fifty adult volunteers for thirty hours of fasting. Over the two days, participants learned about injustice and global poverty, raised money for famine relief, took part in several community service projects, and explored new spiritual practices. It was extraordinary every time.

It was also insane.

I remember trying to pitch this to the parents for the first time and one of the mothers, who was very much trying to support me, gently said, "Kate, when my girl is having a hard time, I ask myself if she is HALT: hungry, angry, lonely, or tired. You are going to gather a bunch of teenagers together, teach them about systemic injustice, deny them food, and keep them up for two days straight? I'm concerned this might not go well." But the Lord is faithful to fools and children, as they say. Our youth were children, and we were fools, and these annual events became exceptionally generative and fruitful. However, they had enormous logistical challenges and were very hard on us as leaders.

One year at about three or four in the morning, when we had finally tricked and cajoled the last young person to sleep, we leaders gathered to debrief the day and troubleshoot challenges ahead. We were fasting along with the young people, so we were tired and hungry and regretting every significant life decision that led us to this point. I don't remember what problem we were trying to solve—probably the logistics of transporting groups of the kids to worship with each of the participating congregations the next day—but I broke down in ridiculous, uncontrollable tears.

Sarah looked at me and then at her husband and said, "Mark, come over here and make yourself small." Her husband instantly laid down on the floor and curled himself into a ball. The sight of this enormously tall, strong hospice chaplain contorting himself into a ball was so unexpected and ridiculous that my exhausted tears morphed into hysterical laughter. It had nothing to do with anything, it didn't make any sense, but it was hilarious.

She explained that whenever she got overwhelmed studying Greek or Tillich in seminary, Mark would get up from the table and curl himself into a ball on the floor for no reason at all. It was ridiculous, and every time it made everything seem both better and possible. Sometimes, when we really love someone, we make ourselves silly for the sheer joy of delighting them. We will dance around. We will make ourselves small.

The American dream is to work hard, get what you deserve, take credit for it, and become exactly who you desire to be. The American dream makes limits of any kind anathema to us, and this dream has invaded the church like the lantern fly, stripping our collective theological imagination. In the aftermath, the church most closely resembles an industrial, idol-manufacturing plant.

In the beginning, so the Genesis story goes, humans lived in community with God in paradise: working in the garden, taking walks in the cool of the evening, completing one another in the interdependent thriving of blessedness that is shalom. God who spun the stars into the sky and the stella bacteria into the microcosmos, God who settled the Leviathan into the sea and decorated the Temple with the nests for the sparrows, God who made Adam from the dust and Eve from Adam and breathed his own breath into both of them: that same God told them they were free to eat from any tree in the garden, including the tree of life, with the exception of the fruit of the tree of the knowledge of good and evil. They were prohibited from consuming that one kind of fruit.

"That's stupid," agreed Adam and Eve, the mother and father of us all. "Why should anything be withheld from us? Why should we not have every single thing we desire? Look at all that we've been given, whatever God is holding us back from must be even better! Who can stop us from doing what we want? Why shouldn't we do what seems good and right in our eyes? Who is this 'God' to tell us no? What has he ever done for us except deny and deprive us? This 'God' says we must not, and so, of course, we must."

You can think this is a myth about an apple if you want to. You can say that because it has been twisted into misogyny, it is nothing but a vicious lie. At times I've certainly dismissed it that way. But now, after years of serving children and youth and then mothering my own, I see it is heartachingly true—and not just for the kids I love but for myself. There is a wise and necessary part of me that views human authority with real suspicion and mistrust. Reflexively, this shapes my relationship with God.

But in my community we sing a song about the steadfast faithfulness of God, tracing it in our own lives. The chorus slows us down and calls us to remember all the goodness of God we've encountered, not in the pages of a Bible but in our own ordinary days. By the unmerited and offensively generous grace of God, this is true testimony.

Still, a small voice whispers, at three in the morning or in traffic jams or when I am just not getting what I want and certainly deserve: Just because God has been good and faithful to me in the past, why should I trust God with my future? Why should I pattern my life according to the life of the Word made flesh Jesus? Why shouldn't I get what I want? Why shouldn't I do what seems best in my own eyes? Who knows best what's good for me: God or me? The answer is obviously me. It takes me less than a minute to become my own god.

When Jesus tells us we must become like little children to enter into the kingdom, he's not requiring us to become powerless, selfless, little machines. He's not telling us that God wants us to be seen and not heard. He's not calling us to fearful, unquestioning obedience.

We have been so collectively wounded by human hierarchies that we reject anything less than full status and maturity. We cannot stomach being less than, even less than God. The irony is that when we embrace our status as children of God, all human hierarchies are instantly dismantled. There is no more striving, no more proving, no more seeking approval or status.

Jesus isn't telling us we are less than. He is telling us that we are cherished children free to play with abandon in the shelter of God's limits. He is telling us we immediately enter into his realm once we know that we are treasured beloved ones. We can only fully enter once we understand that we are the claimed children of an endlessly good and gentle God. Jesus is inviting us to live unapologetically as we actually are.

Beloved and safe children are free to learn and grow. They aren't paralyzed with dread when they realize that they do not have what they need; they know they can turn to their mother when they run out. They know they can run to their father when they are in trouble. They are curious, not offended or troubled, when they encounter mystery, because they know they were made to learn. They venture out fearlessly, knowing that they will always be welcomed home. They are confident that they will always get a fresh start. They know they will always be sheltered in their weakness, and never mocked or despised for it. They know they are the apple of their father's eye. They know the hairs on their heads are numbered. They know that all they have to do to please their mother is to keep on breathing.

Beloved and cherished children are not wounded by their own limited understanding. They are protected from their desires to put their hands on the bright red glow of the stove. Their parents' greater wisdom shelters and nurtures them. They have no need to pretend they already know what they are learning.

When beloved and safe children grow overwhelmed, when they feel worthless and defeated, the words of lullabies well up in their souls: *You are loved, you are worthy, you are beautiful, you are becoming, lift up your head, you have nothing to fear.*

So many of us bear mother or father wounds in our souls. We carry the deep ache of needing to know that the ones who gave us life are pleased with us. That they see us, our whole unvarnished selves, beauty and brokenness, and they love not who we could or should be but who we actually are. Many of us carry a deep wound because we have sought but not found that approval from our parents.

As I look at my own cherished children, I see it from the other side as well. How my own wounds, fears, and anxieties hinder me in the one act of faithfulness I owe my daughters—to love them fully and freely. Becoming like a child and entering God's kingdom means this well of longing is filled to overflowing. Our mothering, fathering God sees and delights in us. Our parents and children become our siblings; we can release them to God's care and delight in them as they are. They cannot supply our deepest needs, but they no longer have to.

Beloved and treasured children look to the future with joyful hope. They have an unshakable, innate dignity. They are not scared of what is unfamiliar. They are undeterred by threats. They have nothing to prove. They are free to become all they were created to be. The cruelest lies of the culture cannot penetrate the shield of sacred family love, be it the immediate, extended, or christological family—or all three. Well-loved children know that they will always have access to goodness, joy, and grace. They know there is something delightful in being small. They are unencumbered and wildly free. They are eager to join in the unfamiliar dance.

* * *

How, then? How do we come back to this place of delightful, free, and fearless childlikeness? How can we return to a place many of us have never been? Perhaps by "wasting" time in every child's first home: imagination.

Try stealing away to a quiet place within your own soul for a moment. Here in the beginning, just *pretend* you believe that God is good and strong and tender and delights in all the parts of you. Imagine God is near, leading you through the valley of the shadow of death, toward green pastures and still waters. Imagine God is showing you how to live fearing no evil, teaching you to trust the power of the goodness of her presence. Imagine God taking you by the hand, patiently teaching you to live abundantly. Imagine that God is delighted at the chance to be with you while you learn to live by grace.

I helped each of our daughters learn to ride a bike without training wheels. It was a different parenting odyssey each time. We bribed and cajoled our oldest out of her training wheels. She was fearful and made us promise that we would always run alongside her, ready to catch her if she fell. She demanded our support long after she needed it. Anxious that she'd never learn to trust herself, I teased (read: shamed) her into taking off on her own. It's not my favorite parenting memory. But at the time, I was focused on how quickly I could get her to learn. I thought I was in a race against other parents teaching their kids to ride bikes. I was losing. I saw her ability to ride a bike as an indicator of my parenting skills, and I had lots to prove.

My middle daughter demanded we remove her training wheels as soon as she noticed that her bike looked different from her big sister's. We took her out to a big parking lot to learn unobstructed, but when we started to jog alongside her and hold her steady, she began to scream, "Let me go! *Let me go!* I already know! I won't fall!"

I tried to tell her that she wasn't ready. I was calm until I wasn't. But she was insistent, and we argued. I knew our hands were holding her up, but she was certain our grip was holding her back. Finally, we did let her go, and she did fall, over and over again, until frustration and skinned knees became unbearable and she gave up for the day. But as soon as the bandages fell off, she climbed back on, confident she didn't need any support as she learned, certain she wouldn't fall, angry again that we were holding her back and slowing her down. And she fell, again and again and again. Until she didn't. It was a battle of wills. She won. She learned how to ride a bike—but not, I thought, the right way.

My youngest daughter currently believes she will never learn to ride her bike without training wheels. The deep irony is that she already can. She takes off like a rocket, straight and steady, but then she remembers she fell the last time, tries to stop, and crashes. She's learning how to ride, and I'm finally learning how to teach. So this time, I'm not arguing. I'm not teasing or shaming. I'm not taking away support she says she needs or giving support she says she doesn't. Right now, she doesn't want to try again, so we're waiting until she does. Because the thing is, the third time around I finally understand my role in this process. She already has everything she needs to master this skill. She was made for this. I'm not teaching her anything. I'm just here to support her and bear witness while she discovers what her body can do.

Jesus tells us we can only enter the kingdom like a little child. I wonder if the best way to imagine that is to picture the way a wise and loving parent teaches a child to ride a bike without training wheels. The child might be certain she will only ever fall, that what other kids can do will always be beyond her. Or the child might think that he doesn't need any help or support at all. Either way, over and over again, the parent gives the child what is needed: a helmet, a bike, and a wide-open space. It looks like a father helping his child climb back on the bike, again and again. It looks like a mother putting Spider-Man Band-Aids on skinned knees. It looks like a parent sitting calmly, waiting until the child is ready to try again, whether that takes minutes or months.

We enter the kingdom of God like a child learns to ride a bike without training wheels. Not knowing how to do this thing but knowing God is confident that we can. Remembering God is certain we are able to do this thing we've never done before. Hearing the

Spirit's whisper telling us over and over again that this was made for us, we were made for this. God knows us better than we know ourselves. God lets us set the pace of learning. There is no too fast, there is no too slow. We have all the time in the world. At first we pedal, believing all we are learning is how to fall. God watches with delight, knowing that what we are really learning is how to fly.

We spend so much time focusing on what we believe about God. Perhaps, as a part of reclaiming our holy childlikeness, we should spend equal time focusing on what God believes about us.

CONCLUSION

WHEN YOU ARE a pastor, people expect you to have a biblical hero: some person you meet in Scripture and aspire to emulate—a journey to copy, a map to follow. Maybe David, the warrior poet, the "man after God's own heart" (don't think about the rape and murder). Maybe Moses, the great liberator and leader (don't notice the murder and massacres). Maybe Abram, who heard from a God he did not know and left behind everything he did; he held nothing back, not even his only son (only, he had two sons, until he decided he didn't—don't think about that either). Or Joshua, rushing into the land of giants, ever choosing this day who he would serve. (And faithfully practicing genocide. Hey, look at the size of those grapes!)

But because I am a *lady pastor*, people expect me to pick a girl. Perhaps Sarah, who laughed but then got with the program (don't worry about the sex trafficking of Hagar and the casting her away to die part). Or Miriam, who sang a song one time (don't worry about the racist "don't marry outside of our race" part). Or Ruth, who had the kind of love for Naomi that we'd call codependent if it were found anywhere else but Scripture (and whatever you do, *don't* study the euphemism for "feet" in the Hebrew Bible). Personally, I don't talk about Esther at all because I hate her passive, subservient guts. None of these worthy or appropriate ones speak to me, even when I sanitize out the profane parts of their stories—parts that Scripture does its damnedest to preserve for us.

When I was in seminary, my preaching professor told all of us that if we kept our eyes open, we'd meet every single person in Scripture in the pews of our congregations. That was too delicious a theory not to test, and I've kept my eyes open ever since. I've worked with

Saul, whose charisma was as legendary as his mood swings. I've officiated the funeral for the prodigal father whose daughter never came home. I've sat vigil with Hannah as she drunkenly cried for hours, pleading with God to let her carry a baby to term. I've rage cleaned with Martha while venting about the Marys who were too spiritual to wash dishes after the potluck. I've ducked calls from a community activist whose zeal for justice and contempt for the hypocrisy of the people of faith was expressed in tirades so profane, I gained sympathy for the soldiers who threw Jeremiah into the pit.

It didn't occur to me, until decades into my ministry, to wonder if I, too, had a role in the story. That even if I didn't want to pick a biblical hero, I ought to view my own life with as much curious reverence as I viewed the lives of my congregants. I started to wonder which part of the biblical story most closely echoed my own.

At first I struggled to notice my own life as intentionally as I studied the lives of my congregants. I hesitated to seek intersections between my own story and the biblical witness, because I knew I would find them. And I knew, because the Bible tells the truth about humanity, that I wouldn't always be flattered by what I found.

Was I Jonah, petulant and prideful, resenting God's mercy toward those I hated? Was I Peter, boldly walking on water one moment, fearfully sinking the next? Was I the confident, rich, young scholar, full of right answers and earnest desires for salvation but ultimately too attached to comforts and advantages to cast off completely and follow Jesus into the kingdom? Of course, in my worst moments, I am all those people. But I wondered if there was also a person in Scripture whose life might be a sort of spiritual map guiding me into who I am becoming in Christ.

And then it came to me: Jehoshaphat.

* * *

I wouldn't call Jehoshaphat my hero, but I recognize his soul like I recognize my own face in the mirror. In *Grey's Anatomy*-speak, he's my person. He once prayed a prayer—"Lord, we do not know what to do, but our eyes are on you"—that has become my own. At first, I prayed it sheepishly and reluctantly. Now I lift it up wholeheartedly and unceasingly.

If you're looking, you'll find Jehoshaphat's story along with the stories of all the other kings of Israel and Judah preserved in 1 and 2 Chronicles. Nobody ever reads Chronicles unless they are part of some "read the Bible in one year" plan, and even those folks don't read Chronicles because they've usually given up by the middle of Leviticus. You don't hear about Chronicles in church. You won't find much of it quoted on T-shirts or coffee mugs. This is because, as a whole, it is the opposite of inspiring. At first glance, anyway.

There aren't any happily-ever-after endings in Chronicles. David becomes king and his family falls apart. With the labor of enslaved humans, his son Solomon builds an ornate Temple to the God who liberated his ancestors from slavery. The promised land splits into two kingdoms, sparking a vicious cycle of civil wars, and then we get reports of the men lucky or violent enough to seize the throne. King so-and-so ascended the throne of his fathers, he did evil in the sight of the Lord, he had sons, he died, and his son such-and-such succeeded him as king. Rinse and repeat. With very rare exceptions, it's really just the same story over and over again.

Except when it isn't.

Jehoshaphat was king of Judah, and the theological consensus about him is *meh*. He wasn't great, but he wasn't the worst. According to Jehu the seer, "You love the wicked and hate those who love the Lord, therefore the wrath of God is against you. Yet there is some good in you for you have rid the land of Asherah poles and you have your heart set on seeking the Lord" (2 Chron 19:2–3; my translation). Jehoshaphat isn't a hero, but he also can't quite manage being a villain. He isn't who he should be, but he is better than average. He muddles along just slightly above the middle, getting some things really wrong and a few things almost right.

The name Jehoshaphat is a complete declarative sentence. The Hebrew word means "Yahweh is judge." But Jehoshaphat's legacy is far from definitive. Was he faithful to God? Sort of, in some things, in some seasons. He loved God, except for the parts of God he rebelled against. He opposed evil, and he also condoned it. It's strangely fitting that his name became bizarrely preserved as a G-rated colloquialism—"Jumping Jehoshaphat!"—used by those too timid or intimidated to curse. Jehoshaphat never managed to pick a side. His name either signifies God's absolute authority or the unsatisfying compromise you make when you really want to cuss but in a way that won't offend Aunt Mabel.

Still, King Jehoshaphat is managing well enough, until the day messengers inform him that, suddenly, the country is surrounded by the armies of Moab, Ammon, and Edom. These armies are huge. Singularly they could overpower Jehoshaphat's forces. Together they are Armageddon assembled at the border, poised on the brink of a coordinated attack. Somehow, without anyone noticing, all the worst-case scenarios have converged.

The people will be utterly destroyed unless Jehoshaphat, who's not that impressive on his best days, can manage to save the day. He's the king, but he's nobody's savior. Kings were responsible for leading the nation militarily. But even David, at the height of his powers, might have faltered in the face of this challenge, and Jehoshaphat is no David. Now the people face a challenge more extreme than even their most celebrated king encountered. And it's Jehoshaphat who is on the throne, a derivative king—a copy of a copy of a copy of a man of God. The nation, the faith, and life itself are existentially at risk, and for such a time as this, Jehoshaphat is not adequate. Yet there is no one else. All eyes are upon him. What is he going to do about it?

And so this milquetoast, mediocre king makes a bizarre and vulnerable choice. He declares a fast and calls people from every town in Judah to join him in inquiring of the Lord. As a military strategy, it's suicide. As a spiritual response, it's offensive. Maybe the prayers of a righteous man availeth much, but Jehoshaphat wasn't even that righteous. To be clear, in this moment of crisis, the king, whose main job is to rally the troops and lead the army in battle—*this* king, who's not even that holy—makes the tactical decision to pray.

For a long time as a pastor, I was never *that* desperate. I prayed. Of course, I prayed. I prayed with people who came seeking counsel. I prayed sincerely but ceremonially during weddings and funerals. I prayed original liturgical prayers in Sunday morning worship. I meant those prayers.

But when problems came up, which they did with insane frequency, I didn't pray; I worked. I read books and went to conferences and attended meetings. I made plans and organized programs and mediated disputes. I taught classes and recruited volunteers and wrote grants. I developed trainings and mentored leaders and wrote newsletter articles. I served and I studied, and I stressed and stayed awake at night, worrying about tasks I'd left undone, names I'd forgotten, people I'd offended. I wrote monster to-do lists. Every once in a while, I'd remember my friend's "Jesus Is Coming. Look Busy!" T-shirt. I still didn't understand the joke, but I knew I didn't appreciate it.

Every month, a church leader would read a treasury report, which consisted solely of an announcement of how many more months we could survive running our deficit budget, our own personal doomsday clock. The voices were telling me we were surrounded. What was against us was immeasurably greater than what was in us. Our challenges would have been daunting to the most seasoned, skilled, and faithful pastor, and I was none of those things. There weren't literal armies surrounding our church, but the forces amassed against us were insurmountable. I was desperate enough to work to become a better leader, a better Christian, a better pastor, but not desperate enough to pray. I was not yet Jehoshaphat.

My friend Eulando was, though. Invited to serve on a denominational committee tasked with reversing the trend of declining churches, he sat for weeks around a table with other pastors and church leaders, and they studied the numbers: how many churches were closing, the toxic ratio of funerals to baptisms, how few new members were joining, how many congregations were unable to pay their pastors or their dues to the national church, how long it had been since a new church had been planted. It was grim.

And then it was time to do something: to fight, to strategize, to make a plan to turn the tide. The ideas came fast and furiously: Hire a consultant, launch an initiative, put on a conference.

That's when my friend Eulando went full Jehoshaphat: "We need to devote significant time to prayer and seeking God's guidance." Eulando went on to explain that he wasn't talking about a moment of silent centering at the beginning of the meeting or the quickie prayer at the end of a session. He wasn't suggesting they meditate on relevant biblical passages.

No. He was proposing months of sustained, urgent, intercessory prayer, calling leaders from every congregation to join them, perhaps inviting members from every church to fast while praying together.

Everybody looked at him like he had suggested doing karaoke at a funeral. "Haven't you been paying attention?" they were thinking. "The church is in crisis, this is an emergency, and there's no way we'll survive if we don't take drastic action. This is not the time to pray; we need to do something."

But Eulando understood the story of mediocre Jehoshaphat; the king who loved the Lord, but not as much as he should; the one who had "some good in him" but also was complicit in the wickedness and syncretism of his day. Jehoshaphat had his faults, but pride wasn't one of them. He wasn't stupid either; he knew his military prowess wasn't saving anyone. So when he found his kingdom surrounded by powerful enemies, he didn't believe in himself. He didn't desperately try harder to become a better king. He had the great and terrible gift of self-awareness. He knew he wasn't good enough or holy enough to control the outcome. He understood God owed him nothing; nevertheless he prayed.

I suspect Jehoshaphat thought it wouldn't make a difference. But he prayed anyway. He fasted and prayed and invited everyone to pray with him. Then he led his people out on the battlefield and they knelt down, baring their souls and exposing their necks, and worshiped God. The stakes were too high for anything but vulnerable humility. When all eyes turned to him, he turned all eyes to God. There was only one possible way out: God. And he ended his prayer with those words of sacred desperation: "We know not what to do, but our eyes are on you."

For so long my eyes have been on myself. I was desperate in my belief and sincere in my attempts, and I was determined to go down swinging. Surely, at some point God would step in, reward my efforts, and make everything okay. I would be brave like David, I would be wise like Solomon, I would be long-suffering but steadfastly faithful like Job. I was even willing to be strategically charming like Esther, dang it. Surely somewhere there was a biblical model I could follow, a tweak I could make, a practice I could hone that would turn things around. Surely there was something I could do other than emulate this mediocre king who, when the stakes couldn't be higher, just surrenders the outcome to God and prays?

God hears Jehoshaphat's prayer and sends a message to him through the prophet. "Don't be afraid or discouraged because of this vast army. Because the battle does not belong to you, but to the Lord. Do not be afraid or be discouraged. You will not have to fight this battle. Go out tomorrow to face them in the valley and the Lord will be with you" (2 Chron 20:15–17; my translation).

So the average-on-his-best-days king leads the people into the valley where the battle will take place—and they worship. In naked self-interest, under threat of annihilation, they worship the God they haven't served very well in peace and prosperity. They begin to sing and praise the Lord. And inexplicably, their enemies turn and begin to fight one another. Soon the battlefield is covered in dead bodies, and the bewildered people help themselves to abandoned equipment and plunder the corpses.

I didn't say this was a pretty story or an easy one.

The army and their king were wholly inadequate, but it turned out not to matter. The battle didn't belong to them after all. God delivered them from their enemies and kept all the glory. At the end of that day, nobody thought any better of Jehoshaphat, but they told the story of the power and mercy, the goodness and the mystery of their God. When we teach our children about biblical heroes, we don't include Jehoshaphat's name. That's because he's not the hero of his own story. God is. Perhaps, with holy irony, this makes him the most important biblical hero of all.

When we finally became weary of all our earnest striving and too tired to justify our self-interested serving, Jehoshaphat's story beckons. What if we accept that we aren't good enough to save the day but hold onto the idea that salvation might still be an option? What if we surrender our preferred roles as proxy saviors and adopt Jehoshaphat's posture of vulnerability and holy dependence? What if we accept—and learn to delight in—the fact that our gifts and efforts are small and cannot swing the balance of anything? When we are ready, this story becomes not a how-to guide to be followed but an invitation to wonder.

Maybe God is more than a system to be worked or a reward to be earned or a benign force to be harnessed or appeased. Maybe God will be forever a mystery; but maybe, maybe God is a mystery of goodness, full of grace. Maybe we can learn to trust God when we cannot trust ourselves. Maybe we are meant to ask for help we have not earned. Maybe in the kingdom of God, vulnerability is both wisdom and strength. Maybe we were never called to be excellent game changers who save the day. Maybe Christians serve best not by being anybody's savior, but in being humble enough to have one. Maybe healthy and mature Christians are those who find such life-giving rest in the vast goodness of God that they no longer worship worldly greatness or despise smallness in themselves or those around them.

* * *

These days I am joining the priesthood of Jehoshaphat. I am one who scans the horizon and sees nothing but forces to fear. I am no longer foolish enough to believe that I was made for such a time as this. I hope for far more than survival, and I know there is nothing in me to satisfy those hopes. I know myself too well to try to be a hero.

And I'm far enough along now to know that all the people standing in the spotlights, all the people surrounded by wealth and affirmation and exceptionalism, aren't sufficient either. Working harder and harder to be more and more like them, buying their books and studying their lives for a secret formula to emulate, isn't the way.

But giving up isn't the way either. Counting the minutes 'til wine o'clock, leveraging all the power I have into advantages for my own dear ones, withdrawing and turning my heart and eyes away, labeling the destruction inevitable as a way of absolving myself of responsibility: That isn't the way either.

I cannot go on as I have, but I also cannot walk away, so I am following Jehoshaphat out into the heart of the fray. Like him, I know that my own choices have empowered the forces that stand against me. I know I am not who I should be, who I could be, who I was created to be. I know that God owes me nothing. But still, I have faith in the goodness of God. I believe that God is a Savior.

And there is enough feeble goodness in me to vulnerably continue loving the church I cannot protect. There is a small, and admittedly self-interested, love in me that hopes in a way of life I've never consciously lived. And now I am here on Jehoshaphat's field, disillusioned and too weary to even pretend to be brave or competent or wise. Now that we've arrived at the last moment, when there are no reasonable options, you might as well worship the goodness of God, because all is lost anyway.

There is an ego-wrestling wisdom that is in me but not of me that throws me down on my face. When you are no longer seeking a hero, or seeking to be a hero, there is something you can do other than give up. You can turn to God and pray a desperate prayer for salvation. And Jehoshaphat's legacy is a shining upside-down kingdom truth: God helps those who stop trying to help themselves. God saves those who stop trying to save themselves. This is not fair, but this is grace. The way is hidden in the king's name. Jehoshaphat means "Yahweh is judge." God decides to save us. Our hope was always hidden in the enigma of God's own name: Yahweh, meaning "I will be who I will be."

Because God isn't out to destroy us—just our illusions: our illusions that we are exceptionally good people, our illusions that our faith guarantees we will get what we believe we deserve, our illusions that our striving and effort are necessary and pleasing to God, our illusions that terrible things will never happen to us, our illusions that abundant life in Christ looks like success. And the biggest illusion of all? That God predestined us for a large, centered, and celebrated life.

All these illusions tell us that we can have control through spiritual hard work. They help us to sleep at night, until they don't. But ultimately, they twist our faith into a noose. They turn life with God into ceaseless striving. Practicing our faith becomes chipping away at an unending spiritual to-do list. There is no rest. Our illusions compel us to work for Jesus. But a disillusioned faith allows us to walk with him, wait on him, hope in him, and rest in him.

I was taught to read my Bible like a choose-your-own-adventure moral guide. Be faithful and adventurous like Abram, be forgiving like Joseph, be prayerful like Hannah, be loyal like Ruth, be brave like David, be wise like Solomon. The authorities told me grace meant I could cultivate all the traits of these biblical heroes and then God would bless me like God blessed them. Our illusions keep us comfortable, docile, and reasonable. But disciples of the risen Lord are none of those things. Our illusions *feel* good, but they aren't good. Illusion is just a pretty word for lie. To be *dis*illusioned, then, is to be set free.

The truth is, we are not in control. No matter how sincerely we believe, no matter how hard we work, there are no guarantees. So many, many, many times, people are faithful, people work hard, people choose the good, and it doesn't turn out okay. We need different reasons to choose good. We need a different motivation for loving and following God other than a fake guarantee that if we do, we'll get what we want. We need to recover a love of goodness for its own sake. A longing for a life with Jesus for the sheer beauty of the thing.

Imagine a way of life that makes weapons obsolete. A way where strangers are welcomed, and hurting people are healed. A way where enemies are reconciled and evil itself is redeemed. A way where those who have enough joyfully share with those who need.

That's not some hippie-dippie dream. That's not a communist manifesto. That's shalom. That's the kingdom of God. The prophets foretold it, Revelation uncovered it, and Jesus says it is, even now, already in our midst. We can believe in that kingdom, regardless of our circumstances. And when we are crushed by our circumstances, it is the only belief that will sustain us.

Disillusioning us, God beckons us deeper into the truth of a wilder, freer faith. The Holy Spirit does not work for us, but we are still free to choose to serve God. Facing collapse, will we pray like Jehoshaphat, not confident in our track record but even at the end caught up by the beauty of God? When we're pretty sure we won't make a difference, will we still choose to serve?

Maybe faithfulness looks like marginal and dying communities, with no hope of surviving and no reason to trust, trusting anyway. Maybe it's people who can't solve the world's problems and are mostly being crushed by them, still opening their mouths to sing of the beauty of God's way and to decry the lies of the world. Maybe it's communities with just enough for today, sharing with their neighbors and so bearing witness to eternity. Maybe it's one person with just enough energy to do the small thing—the thing the world, even the "Christian" world, deems pathetic and embarrassing.

The kingdom of God is not a meritocracy. Jesus's first disciples didn't find his kingdom in what was large and centered and celebrated in their day, and we won't find it in those places in our day either.

If you are where we were, where Jehoshaphat was, surrounded and outnumbered with no hope of survival, I have a three-word map for you: lost, hidden, and small.

Recover what has been lost.
Seek God where God is hidden.
Holiness shines in the small.

The kingdom is not awarded to the powerful or the worthy or the elite. It is sacred lightning that strikes the holy fools who dare to dance before the Lord in the storm. It is found by seekers who cast themselves out into the deep, hoping for a new way. In my own long season of unmooring, I had fears too deep to name. I was afraid that because I didn't receive the goodness of God in the ways I expected to receive it I had been abandoned. I feared that somehow I had forfeited the promises of God.

Sometimes, we really can't go on anymore. We find ourselves lying on the rock in despair, and the heavens open and the rain comes not to mock us but to make us new. Sometimes what feels like the end of everything familiar and good is finally the beginning.

There are a million beautiful, vibrant, and as-yet unimagined ways to come alive in Christ, and one of them is uniquely yours. I pray you hold on as you are becoming. What I know for sure is that you already have everything you need to be faithful to God in this season. Your love for God and for the beloved ones around you can never be lost and is *never* wasted. The glorious eternal end of the story was revealed on the cross: God's shalom has triumphed over all that seeks to destroy. The future is redemption and repair and resurrection, and the future begins here and now. Without our effort, without our awareness, without our permission, the grace of Jesus Christ bears us up, in these days and all the days of our lives.

Come and see.

ACKNOWLEDGMENTS

I DO NOT know who I would be if I did not know the Lord. And I know Jesus because of the ordinary beautiful faithfulness of the seven churches who have received me as Christ's own in every season of my life.

The saints at Strathmoor Presbyterian Church defied Presbyterian policy and baptized me as an infant even though my parents were not members. The saints at Highland Presbyterian Church welcomed me intermittently as an elementary school child, confirmed me as a middle schooler, and, much later, shepherded me through the ordination process. The saints at Crestwood United Methodist Church embraced me as a surly, awkward teenager, surrounded me with the love of Jesus and taught me that I was part of the body of Christ. The saints at Needham Presbyterian Church took me in as a graduate student, gave me my first chance to practice ministry with their children, and showed me extraordinary grace. Fourth Presbyterian Church in South Boston gave me my first call and showed me that church can transcend and transform all earthly divisions. The saints at Cooks Memorial Presbyterian Church in Charlotte called me to minister to their youth and loved me unconditionally, and I am forever grateful to the mothers of that church who supported me in thousands of ways as I became a mother.

Finally, the saints at The Grove Presbyterian Church in east Charlotte took a huge chance on me, accompanied me through our collective death and resurrection, and continue to love me as a friend. You are the church of my dreams, and every day is a gift.

There is no such thing as an ordinary church.

A GUIDE FOR REFLECTION AND DISCUSSION

Author's note: These questions can be used for individual reflection or in a group. The second item in each section contains a brief passage of Scripture for reading and reflection, for those who wish to incorporate Bible study.

Introduction

1. What are your initial thoughts about the author's argument that the North American church has been corrupted and malformed by an invasive and un-Christlike spirituality? Does this contradict or validate your personal experience?
2. Read John 9:1–4. What parts of the story stand out most to you? With whom do you most identify in the text? In verse 39 Jesus says, "For judgment I have come into this world, so that the blind will see and those who see will become blind." To what degree have you experienced a change in vision because of knowing Jesus? Have you ever come to see something differently because of the life and teachings of Jesus?
3. The dominant metaphor of the introduction is the spotted lanternfly, a creature that looks beautiful and harmless but is actually exceptionally destructive. The lanternfly is more dangerous because its beauty attracts us. If something looks good, it is harder to perceive that it is a threat. The author argues that we are naturally attracted to some things (like wealth, power, and praise) that actually are harmful to us and our communities. Do you agree?

4. Is it a paradigm shift for you to consider the way of Jesus lost, hidden, and small? Do those words fit with your expectations of the holy?

1. We Are the Lost Ones

1. Do you have personal experience or cultural familiarity with a particular Christian tradition such as evangelical, mainline, charismatic, Pentecostal, or nondenominational? How did or does that community talk and teach about "the lost"? Do you have an emotional response to the phrase?
2. Read Luke 15:1–3. What images or characters are most important to you? Can you find yourself in any of the parables?
3. The parables that Jesus tells about the lost portray them as intrinsically belonging (the lost sheep is an authentic part of the flock), valuable (the lost coin is worth as much as the other coins), and beloved (the father of the prodigal son does not join the celebration until both of his sons are reconciled to him). If you are part of a faith community, does it reflect the heart of Jesus toward those who are not part of it?
4. Some Christians believe perceiving and labeling any group as the lost is pejorative, offensive, and promotes intolerance and even violence. Do you agree?
5. The author argues that many Christians have lost an essential understanding of the gospel and thus have themselves become the lost. Do you ever identify as lost? How might Christian communities be transformed if, when reading these parables, they saw *themselves* as the lost ones being found by Jesus?

2. Shalom: We All Fare Well

1. What associations do you have with the word *peace*? Do you identify peace as the absence of conflict or the presence of

justice and well-being? Has the pursuit of personal peace or peacemaking been part of your spiritual life?

2. Read Matthew 5:1–11. Which words or phrases stand out to you? Do you identify with any of the beatitudes?
3. The author describes how she initially held a shallow, false mondegreen misunderstanding of peace as the absence of conflict. Have you ever misunderstood a significant spiritual concept like peace or justice? What was the process of unlearning like for you?
4. The author shares how the lost biblical concept of shalom deepened and expanded her understanding of peace. How does shalom differ from the common American cultural understanding of peace?
5. How might recovering an understanding of peace as the presence of shalom change our relationship with injustice and poverty? How might the pursuit of shalom—the mutual interdependent well-being of all creation—influence the way followers of Jesus form relationships with those Jesus identifies as the least of these?
6. If a community of believers recovered a holy passion for shalom, how would that pursuit of true peace change its posture toward institutions and individuals who currently hold power and authority? Do you think a person seeking to be a peacemaker would be celebrated and honored in contemporary American culture?

3. Kinship: We Belong to One Another

1. How have you been taught to understand the word *family*? Who do you consider family? How do you determine whether a person is part of your family? How has this understanding of family helped or hindered you?
2. Read Matthew 12:46–50. What stands out to you? Does this piece of the Jesus story feel like good news to you?

3. North American culture tends to identify family as solely those who are connected to you by binding legal agreement, such as marriage, adoption, or shared genetic material. Do you think this is a faithful way of understanding family?
4. The author argues that Jesus established the church so that humans could rediscover kinship: humanity as one flourishing human family that encompasses individuals of all ethnicities and cultures and transcends and heals all divisions. In what ways do the concepts of kinship and family differ in terms of belonging, inclusiveness, and obligation?
5. Contemporary North American churches tend to be segregated by race and class. Why do you think churches tend to form in this way? What is lost when we accept this as inevitable or even preferable?
6. We tend to care for people we consider family differently than we do for those we don't consider family. How does Jesus's vision of family as kinship with all humans challenge your understanding of family obligations? If you recovered Jesus's vision of family, what challenges would you anticipate? What blessings might it bring?

4. Trinity: Healing from Hierarchy

1. What associations, connotations, or understandings, if any, do you have of the word *trinity*? Does it have any daily relevance to your life or spiritual practice?
2. Read Matthew 3:1–17. Do any parts of the passage trouble you? Does any portion of this story seem especially beautiful to you?
3. What do you see as the advantages and disadvantages of hierarchical organizations in which some individuals have power and authority over other individuals? Are there times where hierarchy is healthy and appropriate?
4. Many churches function as hierarchies. Hierarchies can be expressed in many ways. It could look like a pastor or

spiritual leader with ultimate responsibility and authority over all other community members. It could be a community where certain identity groups have priority and authority over other identity groups. It could be a spiritual community where a small group of lay members hold power over the whole community to control growth and prevent change. What are your thoughts about the appropriateness of hierarchy in Christian community?

5. The author argues that in Jesus's baptism, when he refuses to claim superiority over John and instead makes himself vulnerable to participate in our baptism, Jesus is displaying a new kind of righteousness that disturbs and destroys our orienting principle of hierarchy. Do you agree or disagree?
6. The author proposes trinity as an alternative model of community. In the life of Jesus we see the Oneness of God the Father, Jesus the Son, and the Holy Spirit: interdependently, indivisibly, holy, and whole in one another. There is no forced manipulation, coercion, or threat—only mutual submission, trust, and interdependence. How would a community modeled on the concept of trinity differ from a community modeled on hierarchy? What new challenges would this create? What advantages would such a community have?

5. There Is More Than We Know

1. What are some Christian slogans you've run across in your life? How have you known them to be helpful or harmful? Does the thought that God is more than we can fully know encourage you? Frustrate you? Frighten you?
2. Read Matthew 13:44–46. Do these parables seem like good news to you? What do you visualize when you hear the phrase "seeking the kingdom of heaven"? What does that practically look like? Do you believe Christians need to actually do this?

3. Have you ever experienced the absence or silence of God? If so, how would you describe that experience? What, if any, are the lasting consequences? If you have participated in a Christian community, how did that community support you in that season or prepare you for it?
4. The author believes that the hiddenness of God is a core revelation of Scripture. Do you agree?
5. Mainstream North American Christianity tends to emphasize the instant accessibility and easy comprehensiveness of God. Is this a faithful message? Why are we so drawn to it?
6. How might a church which acknowledges the hiddenness of God be more compassionate, nurturing, tender, and hopeful?

6. Repentance: It's Not What You Think

1. Are you familiar with the word *repent*? What practices do you associate with repentance? What connotations or associations do you have?
2. Read Matthew 4:1–17. The classic definition of repent is to turn away from sin and turn toward God. In the desert, what is Jesus turning away from? What is Jesus turning toward? How is Jesus modeling repentance for us here? In calling us to repent, what is Jesus calling us to turn away from? What is Jesus calling us to turn toward?
3. What are the characteristics of communities that foster healing, growth, and change? What are the characteristics of communities that hinder transformation?
4. What do you imagine a healthy spiritual practice of repentance looks like? What does toxic repentance look like? Have you ever known anyone (or considered yourself to be) too righteous to repent?
5. Why do you think so many North American Christians are unwilling or unable to seriously consider their own culpability? Why do you think members of the recovery community do this so much more successfully?

7. Surrender: I Might Not Get What I Want

1. What positive or negative associations do you have with the concept of *surrender*? What about with *control*?
2. Read Matthew 13:3–23. In the parable, the farmer sows seed indiscriminately. It appears that much of his labor and resources were wasted. In what ways might this story reshape our understanding of what it means to be "successful" Christians? How might this parable challenge us to surrender our desire for control to God?
3. Have you seen or experienced spiritual communities in which surrender is used to justify spiritual abuse? What do you believe a healthy spiritual practice of surrender looks like?
4. The author shared her long-standing fear that surrender was a spiritualized word for apathy, indifference, and giving up. Do you associate surrender with passivity and resignation? Is there such a thing as *active* surrender? What might that look like?
5. Murphy began to understand that her attempt to control what was beyond her control was damaging to herself and others. Do you resonate with the idea that unrealistic expectations for self and others can cause great harm?
6. What does it look like to surrender to God but not necessarily to those who claim God's name or power or authority? Are there ways in which fully surrendering one's life to God can make believers freer to defy injustice and labor for shalom?

8. Failure: We Will Lose. A Lot.

1. Reflect on or share some of your own experiences with loss and failure. Do you associate those moments with shame or guilt? In what ways does it seem appropriate to identify Jesus as a loser? In what ways does it seem inappropriate to identify Jesus as a winner?

2. Read Mark 8:27–37. How does this passage challenge or conform to your understanding of spiritual victory? How should Jesus's question, warning that it is possible to forfeit one's soul while gaining the world, shape our understanding of failure and success?
3. Do you agree with the author's conclusion that the power of Christ is "the power to resist. It is the power to lose"?
4. In what ways is a "win at all costs" Christian culture contradictory to the witness of Christ?
5. Murphy begins this chapter with a list of best-selling books on Christian victory. She then offers the examples of Paul Farmer, Corrie ten Boom, and the nine worshippers at Mother Emanuel AME Church in Charleston, South Carolina, as modern-day saints and martyrs. How do their legacies challenge and expand your understanding of what true victory in Christ entails?

9. Nothing Good Could Happen Here

1. What associations or connotations do you have with the word *small*? What are some things that are generally considered better and more desirable the smaller they are? What are some examples of things that are considered inferior the smaller they are?
2. Read Matthew 13:31–33. Which words or phrases are most important to you? If a young child asked you to explain these parables to them, what would you say? Why might God choose to associate the holy with small things instead of large things?
3. The author writes in this chapter: "Formed by a culture that celebrates corporate mergers, economies of scale, and health care consolidation, we do not know how to imagine a greatness that isn't large and universal." Do you expect that the healthier and more faithful a church is, the larger it will become?

4. In what ways is the small scale of Jesus's life a revelation about the kingdom of God? How does this challenge the teaching of the Christian industrial complex that God resides in whatever is large, centered, and celebrated?
5. Can you think of ways that choosing to live with radical faithfulness to God would lead to a reverence for small things? How might such a reverence restore health and wholeness to Christian communities?

10. Humility: The Church Should Not Be Excellent

1. What associations do you have with the word *humility*? Do you aspire to be humble? Are there any historical or biblical figures you believe exemplify humility?
2. Read Mark 12:38–44. Which person in this passage do you identify with most closely? Where do you find yourself in the story? Jesus warned about the pride and hypocrisy of the religious leaders. What kinds of common Christian practices do you think Jesus would specifically call out today? What do you think about the widow's choice to give her last coins to the Temple treasury? Is there a danger to celebrating this kind of vulnerable generosity?
3. In what ways has an uncritical pursuit of greatness as "excellence" damaged the integrity of the Christian church? Can you think of ways in which our desire to be celebrated as excellent has compromised the witness of the church and caused harm to vulnerable people?
4. Murphy argues that the excellence of Christ is revealed in the cross: "The exceptionalism of Jesus wasn't in the kind of powerful, impressive life we aspire to have; it doesn't look like the excellence we fetishize. Jesus did not overcome. For love's sake, he endured—until he didn't." Do you agree that the cross is the ultimate manifestation of Christian excellence? If so, how might that understanding reshape how contemporary Christian communities define and pursue excellence?

5. Imagine two Christian communities: one that celebrates humility and ordinary faithfulness and one that celebrates excellence and exceptionalism. What kinds of practices and behaviors would be valued in each community? What kinds of people would be drawn to each community? What unique risks and opportunities might each community contain?

11. Grace: The Bread Will Rise

1. Do you have any experience making bread or any other item that uses a starter? Why do you think so many people find it meaningful to make something that they could easily buy?
2. Read Matthew 13:33. In this parable, Jesus describes the kingdom of heaven as yeast that a woman mixes into a large quantity of flour until it transforms all the dough. How is this image like and unlike other images you've encountered about the coming of the kingdom of heaven?
3. What is your basic understanding of grace? Murphy argues that understanding the way yeast transforms its surroundings deepens and expands our understanding of how the grace of God is at work in the world. Do you agree or disagree?
4. Why do you think Jesus chooses leaven as a metaphor for his kingdom when his original audience would have associated it with death and sin?
5. This chapter contains a discussion of the exodus story. Murphy argues that the liberation of the Hebrew people required more than physical separation from Egypt and captivity. The people needed to be rid of the "culture" of oppression as well. What parts of American culture do you believe are healthy and in line with the gospel? What parts of American culture do you think faith communities need to be delivered from?
6. Can churches objectively evaluate the culture of their communities? How can people of faith be intentional about cultivating good culture?

12. Delight: Unless You Become Like a Child

1. What positive and negative characteristics do you associate with childhood? How would you define maturity?
2. Read Matthew 18:1–5. Jesus tells his audience they must change and become like children in order to enter into the kingdom. What qualities and practices do you think Jesus is saying are essential in encouraging disciples to be like a child? What kind of life is Jesus calling us to cultivate here?
3. Murphy argues that healthy childlikeness includes the embrace of limits, a willingness to take risks, eagerness to learn, and the cultivation of delight. Which of these most intrigues you? Challenges you?
4. Do you associate delight with the practice of your faith? Why or why not?
5. What kinds of practical choices might a faith community make if it were intentionally trying to cultivate childlikeness? How might such a church be different from a "typical" American congregation?

NOTES

Introduction

9 ***"upside-down kingdom":*** Donald B. Kraybill, *The Upside-Down Kingdom* (Herald Press, 1990).

Chapter 2: Shalom

33 ***"the mind calcifies around its initial idea":*** Jonathan Rogers, "Knowledge Is Power. France is Bacon," The Habit, May 4, 2021, https://thehabit.co/knowledge-is-power-france-is-bacon/.

Chapter 3: Kinship

45 ***"a child born poor in Charlotte":*** Raj Chetty et al., "Where Is the Land of Opportunity? The Geography of Intergenerational Mobility in the United States," *The Quarterly Journal of Economics* 129, no. 4 (2014): 70.

Chapter 6: Repentance

91 ***"the White Citizen's Councilor":*** Martin Luther King Jr., "Letter from Birmingham Jail," in *Why We Can't Wait* (Harper & Row, 1964), 77.

91 ***"more devoted to 'order'":*** King Jr., "Birmingham Jail," 77.

Chapter 7: Surrender

106 ***"God is nearer to us":*** Julian of Norwich, *Revelations of Divine Love*, trans. Elizabeth Spearing (Penguin Books, 1998), 55.

107 ***"All shall be well":*** Julian, *Revelations*, 125.

107 ***"This was said so tenderly":*** Julian, *Revelations*, 57.

107 ***"It is all that is":*** Julian, *Revelations,* 55.
107 ***"God made it":*** Julian, *Revelations,* 220.
108 ***"You would know our Lord's meaning":*** Julian, *Revelations,* 310.

Chapter 8: Failure

119 ***"We want to be on the winning team":*** Paul Farmer, *To Repair the World: Paul Farmer Speaks to the Next Generation* (Farrar, Straus and Giroux, 2013), 42.